A Writer's San Francisco

A Guided Journey
for the Creative Soul

ERIC MAISEL

Drawings by Paul Madonna

NEW WORLD LIBRARY
NOVATO, CALIFORNIA

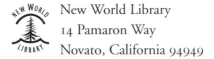 New World Library
14 Pamaron Way
Novato, California 94949

Text design and typography by Mary Ann Casler
Edited by Vanessa Brown
Copyedited by Mimi Kusch and Kristen Cashman

Library of Congress Cataloging-in-Publication Data
Maisel, Eric, 1947–
A writer's San Francisco : a guided journey for the creative soul / Eric Maisel ; Drawings by Paul Madonna.
    p. cm.
Includes bibliographical references and index.
ISBN-13: 978-1-57731-546-9 (hardcover : alk. paper)
  1. San Francisco (Calif.)—Intellectual life. 2. San Francisco (Calif.)—Description and travel. 3. Authorship—Handbooks, manuals, etc. 4. Creative writing. 5. Inspiration. 6. Creative ability. 7. Maisel, Eric, 1947—Travel—California—San Francisco. 8. Authors—Travel—California—San Francisco. 9. Literary landmarks—California—San Francisco. I. Title.
F869.S35M35 2006
917.94'610453—dc22   2006009940

First printing, October 2006
ISBN-10: 1-57731-546-4
ISBN-13: 978-1-57731-546-9

Printed in Hong Kong
Distributed by Publishers Group West

10 9 8 7 6 5 4 3 2 1

For Ann,
who escaped the snow and arrived
at the Owl and the Monkey Café,
where I was waiting

For Natalya and Kira,
our native-born daughters

And for anyone who has left her heart,
or found it,
in San Francisco

Contents

Drawings

꙳

THE VIEW FROM BERNAL HILL

I'M AMERICAN BY BIRTH but an urban writer by nature. My true homes are Paris, London, New York, Tokyo, San Francisco, and the world's resonant cities. I am calmest in a Paris jostle or a Manhattan stampede and edgiest hiking a mountain trail or shopping at Wal-Mart. Everything in the universe may be equally spiritual but not equally congenial to a blue-state person like myself with a horror of orthodoxy and of the grandiosity of ordinary people.

I need cafés, video stores that stock independent films, and bars where everyone is an outsider. I need bookstores, small parks with a comforting glimpse of the concrete beyond, and markets filled with people speaking languages I don't understand. I need a place with more knowing smiles than blank stares and more wry asides than hate-filled sermons. I need a place a full standard deviation above the mean. I therefore choose to live in a village neighborhood of San Francisco where, when a house catches on fire, half the people who rush out to watch are Spanish-speaking ladies and the other half are working-from-home lesbian graphic artists.

The neighborhood is called Bernal Heights. Many of the homes are Edwardians from the post-Earthquake years of 1907 and 1908. This area of San Francisco, anchored by Bernal Hill and bounded on the west by Mission Street, on the east by Bayshore Boulevard, on the south by Alemany Boulevard, and on the north by Cesar Chavez Street, is reputed to have San Francisco's best seismic properties. The well-heeled middle class of 1907 built homes here after the Great Earthquake to take advantage of its bedrock, then abandoned them after World War II, as the Latin population of the Mission District encroached. Gangs flourished, and lesbian couples arrived to buy affordable homes.

Now it is in transition again as "Noe Valley families," young urban professional couples with a small child, an infant, and a dog in tow, further gentrify this sunny spot. These young families come here because of their dogs — a little joke, but a half-truth. Bernal Heights is the dog-friendliest San Francisco neighborhood, since Bernal Hill is an off-leash heaven for dogs and their masters. The Hill boasts 360-degree views of San Francisco and dogs by the dozens, trained to be civilized at local dog manner classes. For the dogs it is a mixed blessing: very little poison oak but many foxtails.

Bernal Hill soars five hundred feet above the surrounding roofs of

Victorians and Edwardians. You can spy the Golden Gate Bridge to the west, Mount Diablo to the east, and all of the Mission and Downtown directly in front of you. It is the perfect place to watch the fog roll in and the last place the fog gathers. People come here from all over the city to watch the Fourth of July fireworks, as might we, if fireworks moved us.

Ours is an Edwardian flat, the second floor of a two-family home, that lives large at 950 square feet. It has a double parlor, that traditional Edwardian feature, a sleeping bedroom, a bedroom/study, a single bathroom, and a large eat-in kitchen that we use as our primary living space. With its tall ceilings, generous windows, good light, and million-dollar view, the kitchen is where my wife, Ann, and I drink wine and catch up. We have a pair of director's chairs by the window, a small table in between, and greenery, freeways, and the Bay beyond.

Since it faces east, the kitchen is sunniest in the morning; as the earth moves, the double parlor at the western end of the flat begins to warm up. In the afternoon the living room sofa is the place to nap — if we napped. We have a string of small Christmas lights wrapped around the banister, one white orchid on a stereo speaker, and Ann's raku vases on the tables. The street outside is sunny and windy, the doorbell has a ghost in it and rings of its own accord once every two weeks, and my mother's cane, which she uses on visits, doubles as sculpture.

To see my creativity-coaching clients, I walk down the hill a block and then head west three short blocks to Progressive Grounds Café. I pass the upscale vegetarian restaurant, the Catholic church, the senior center, the yoga studio, the blues bar with live music, the Italian bistro where we are mocked for ordering so little (one pizza to share and two glasses of wine), and Red Hill Books, named for the time when Bernal Hill was a hotbed of labor organizing and Communist sympathizing.

In good weather, which is virtually year-round, I meet with clients out back, where a two-level patio smelling of jasmine is home to thirty-something Bernal ladies-who-lunch, delicately munching on the best falafel, hot-pressed in phyllo dough rather than stuffed in pita bread, and to students studying. There is always sun, and there is always shade; the Arabic torch music playing inside doesn't reach outdoors; and the stillness, punctuated by light conversation, is palpable.

This is the right place for a coach to meet with a writer. It is also the right place to write. It has a perfect tattooed Zen ambience, a place where body piercings and inner calm meet, where an idea, any idea — a really stupid one, a salacious one, a radical one, an excellent one — is supported by strong coffee, a brick fireplace filled with toys, and a shelf of free books to borrow or steal. Nature gives us thirty years or a hundred, a quill pen or its equivalent, and odd thoughts that need to settle on paper or else turn to dust. In Bernal Heights, they settle nicely.

2.

THE BOHEMIAN INTERNATIONAL HIGHWAY

SAN FRANCISCO AND PARIS are sister cities. They are not connected by architecture, class structure, or climate. They are not connected by their shellfish preferences (in San Francisco it is crab, in Paris it is mussels), their history (Wild West provincial versus urbane royal), or their museums (San Francisco has no Louvre, Musée d'Orsay, or even Pompidou). They are connected by being two of the world's very few bohemian meccas. Each is an important, well-marked stop on the bohemian international highway.

In "The Beat Generation and San Francisco's Culture of Dissent," Nancy Peters explained:

> The idea of bohemia caught the imaginations of writers in early San Francisco with Henri Mürger's *Scènes de la Vie Bohème* (1844), which depicted life in the Latin Quarter of Paris. Although class society in San Francisco bore little resemblance to that of Paris, the city's writers were not blind to the obvious attractions of la vie bohème and reveled the nights away in Montgomery Street bars and restaurants. A bohemian community developed in the 1880s and 1890s around the intersections of Pacific, Washington, Jackson, and Montgomery Streets. When the Montgomery Block building emptied out, artists and writers moved in. Over the years, more than 2,000 of them have lived there, among them Ambrose Bierce, Jack London, Frank Norris, Margaret Anderson, and Kenneth Rexroth.

The bohemian ideal hardly parses, since it is made up of contradictory urges. There is the urge to feast and indulge, the urge to wildness. At the same time there is the urge to witness for the culture and to speak truth to power, the urge to seriousness. There is the garret urge for solitude and the café urge for messy interaction. But even if these urges clash, producing a novelist who would love to witness for the culture if he weren't currently blacked out from vodka or a poet who would love to be capturing grace on her laptop if she didn't have Grace in her lap, a coherent picture emerges, as coherent as a Cubist painting.

It is a picture of a wild, serious bohemian with few natural habitats, one of which is Paris, one of which is San Francisco. To be sure, she may have to spend years in some uncongenial place in order to tend to her dying father or pursue her nonwriting career, she may fail to break free of her birth community and never leave the confines of her town, she may be seduced into living here or confused into living there — in short, she may find himself far from her natural habitat, pacing her cage like a lion in a zoo. But she knows where she ought to be.

The tourist says, "I love San Francisco! Fisherman's Wharf, you know, and the sourdough bread! Oh, and the Golden Gate Bridge!" The writer says, "I love San Francisco" and then shakes his head. What he loves are its traditions and permissions. He loves what City Lights Bookstore represents, its history as a Beat supporter and safe haven that is at least as poignant as Paris's Shakespeare & Company's. He loves the roasting coffee smells of North Beach and the fact that he can write freely here, that his freedom is protected, if not guaranteed.

He loves the iconography of the Summer of Love and the Free Speech Movement, the protests, the tear gas, the symbolic rebellion, the rock and the jazz, the Jefferson Airplane, the radical energy that, unlike its Parisian expression, was not dogmatic Communism but the expression of basic constitutional principles of the sort that terrify politicians. It is now fashionable for almost everyone, hippies included, to shake their heads at that period and say, "Bad trip, man!" Revisionist history has it that there were no principles involved, just acid, debauched sex, and a kind of extended spring break. But revisionist history has it wrong. For a little while America had partisans.

The writer loves the fog as it pours in; he loves the sun when the fog pours out. The rest of California is Beach Boys country, but San Francisco has that moody thing going, those blues notes wrapped in moisture, an atmosphere that tempers California dreaming and makes life more real. But he loves the sun, too, that Frisbee-tossing, forehead-baking golden sun that prevents the loss of eight months of the year to winter. The fog brings reality, but it is still a California reality, one spent outdoors the whole year round.

Maybe he can't say what he loves — maybe it is just a feeling in his heart. It is a feeling that a writer gets in Paris, so powerful that I felt compelled to write a book about it. It is a feeling that a writer gets in Greenwich Village, on a bench in front of Keats's house in Hampstead in the north of London, in the darker parts of any city where outsiders and artists roam, in places where a pen is a sacred object and not something to be feared or scorned. It is a feeling essentially about freedom; secondarily about creation; and together about the freedom to bleed art.

There is a bohemian international highway whose rest stops are separated by long distances and legions of philistines. All along the way writers will wave to you and cry, "Say hello to San Francisco when you get there!" They know that you are going home. It is their home, too, one of their homes, and more like home than the place where they currently reside. It is certainly possible to live in a place where diversity means two or three kinds of orthodoxy. We have all lived in such places for as long as we could tolerate them. But how we itch to escape them and return home to a place like San Francisco.

✺

3

SOUTH OF MARKET

DATELINE 1966. When I wheeled my armored personnel carrier down the rutted road between grassy minefields I felt the joy that only a nineteen-year-old can feel, a cigarette between his lips and a 30-caliber machine gun poised behind his ear. I should have been in the higher turret, manning that machine gun and monitoring the other three armored personnel carriers in the platoon, since I was acting platoon sergeant. But as acting platoon sergeant I got to designate myself as driver. I just loved to wheel that beast down those Korean back roads.

I have personally never met a Republican who served in the army. I'm sure there are some — there must be, as a statistical matter. All the Republicans I've ever met, including those in my extended family, would have loved to serve, except that some darned thing or another prevented them from raising their hands. I am not saying that they were cowards, hypocrites, or liars. But I am surprised at how small an effort they made to overcome their circumstances and land themselves in a nice pair of fatigues. Given their rhetoric, I would have thought they would have tried harder.

Conversely, it is funny how often bohemians enlist. Maybe it is a form of irony. Maybe it is about adventure. Maybe it is our way of acquiring experience. Maybe we have nothing better to do, having flunked out of college or arrived at some equivalent empty moment. Maybe, though in love with freedom, we also love to march. Maybe we actually care about the "American experiment" and would like to see it continue. Who can say? I can only speak for myself: for some set of reasons I wandered into the recruiting office on Times Square one summer day in 1965 and enlisted.

So it was that I ended up at Fort Ord, an army post two hours south of San Francisco on the Monterey Peninsula, where I did my advanced infantry training during the winter of 1965 and the spring of 1966. Now it is a campus of the California college system, but then it was the place where you got ready for Vietnam. During the week I would fire recoilless rifles, grenade launchers, and machine guns; on Friday evenings I would head for San Francisco. Sometimes I hitchhiked with a buddy, and sometimes I took the special bus, filled with GIs, that ran express from Fort Ord to the Greyhound Bus Terminal south of Market, dead square in wino land.

I stayed in fleabag hotel rooms from which, in the fifties, Beat writers moved laterally to equally grim working-class quarters. Jack Kerouac described his room and his mental state in "October in the Railroad Earth," published in 1960: "And there's my room, small, gray in the Sunday morning, now all the franticness of the street and the night before is done with, bums sleep, maybe one or two sprawled on the sidewalk with empty poorboy on a sill — my mind whirls with life, my whole soul and concomitant eyes looking out on this reality of living and working in San Francisco with that pleased semi-loin-located shudder, energy for sex changing to pain at the portals of work and culture and natural foggy fear."

I wasn't writing yet. I was about to turn nineteen and hadn't a clue about life. The previous year I'd flunked out of college, gone on a road trip, and then enlisted. Coursing through me was the raw stuff of youth that manifested as pure enjoyment of firing weapons, a trickster urge to shoplift and give the loot away, and, of course, sexual desire. In a few months I would be in Asia. I knew that I was going there, knew that I was in limbo, knew without quite knowing it that everything becomes surreal while you wait to ship out.

I walked Market Street. Like tourists and locals today, I couldn't decide if Market Street was San Francisco's main street. If it was, with its discount stores, McDonald's, and grim, littered, unremarkable ordinariness, it lowered the city in your estimation. For me, it was San Francisco, and when I veered off it I veered south, toward the homeless and the lost. Now South of Market has multiple meanings, including once-prospering and now-defunct dot-coms, leather bars, and swank designer hotels, museums like the San Francisco Museum of Modern Art and the Contemporary Jewish Museum, and enough culture to earn it a fancy new SoMa appellation (which, however, no San Franciscan uses). Then it mostly meant down-and-out.

I knew seedy San Francisco first. Probably most writers who come here come here poor and know the Tenderloin better than Pacific Heights and noodle restaurants better than the Garden Court. Market Street seemed a step down from the Lower East Side, and South of Market, with its winos and derelicts sleeping head-to-foot like daisy chains, felt like Damon Runyan gone really sour. Some nights I would have to jam a chair under the doorknob against the alcoholic commotion in the corridors. Our barracks at Fort Ord, with its polished floors (because we buffed them) and its clean urinals (because we scoured them) seemed luxurious by comparison.

Could I have lived and written South of Market? Who can say? In the history of writing, writers have come from every class and circumstance. It is a trick of dualistic thinking to say that only the poor writer, steeled in the streets, will write, or that only the comfortable writer, not worried about starving, will continue to write. The fact of the matter is that the only writer who will write is the writer who writes. He will write one-armed, blind, or with a billion in the bank. He will write in a good suit or naked at his makeshift desk. He likely will die younger if he is poor, for all the obvious reasons, but that is a separate matter. If he is a writer he will write, whether atop Nob Hill or South of Market.

4.

THEME PARTY

I WAS THROWING A LITTLE PARTY at our Bernal Heights flat for a visiting publisher, someone with whom I had a long history. She had been my editor fifteen years earlier, one of two editors on my first nonfiction book. Then she went back to school, into the master's program at San Francisco State, to hone her fiction-writing skills. During that interlude I occasionally attended the salons she hosted at her apartment in the foggy Richmond District, so far west that it was almost in Japan. Then she bought a publishing house in Boston and published me. She was going to be in town, and I rounded up some folks for a get-together.

I invited a novelist who was also head of a city department. I invited a novelist who was an investment banker. I invited a novelist who was executive director of an environmental nonprofit. I invited a children's book author who worked in Silicon Valley as a software project manager. I think you get the drift. Except for one jazz pianist who, with a working husband, probably didn't count, no one lived on his or her art. Everyone had a day job, some quite fancy.

It is an interesting, poignant matter to contemplate the fact that so many artists are masquerading as investment bankers, nonprofit directors, and software project managers. How many business calls are conducted by people who would throw the whole shebang into the river, whatever it is they are selling, buying, or negotiating, for a decent chance at a garret? Could it be that there are ten million writers in America, all in disguise, all going to work every day looking quite Stepford?

This means many things, but what it meant this particular Saturday evening to this crowd of professionals was that they could throw off the costumes they wore during the day and stand, laughing and naked, as artists. They could wind up the narrow stairs to the main (and only floor) of our flat and shed the numbers on their speed dial, the number of this lawyer and that board member. They could move from forced day smile to a smile at once brighter and more musing. They could grab a glass of wine, sigh, and breathe. The baklava was just a bonus.

The party was a great success, and not only at the level of canapés and networking. For two hours, guests got to shed the burden of maintaining a false face. The environmental executive director could gleefully exclaim, "F*#k all the birds I'm protecting! I just want to sit on my

bed in my pajamas and write." The city department head could announce, "I go to Paris every year and rent a studio for a month. Isn't
that heaven?" The investment banker could murmur, "No one here
talks about what they own or what they bought. I'm never leaving."

They could be themselves. That was the theme of the party. All day
long, Monday through Friday, and many Saturdays and Sundays, they
were unrecognizable to themselves, exiles from paradise making money
in high-rises, returning one phone call after another with little joy or
genuine interest. They were good at what they did — was that the secret curse? Would they have been better off a little more addled and living on SSI? In any event, for two hours they could shed their grown-up
identities and love life.

In one corner a novelist pitched a goofy nonfiction idea to a recep-
tive editor. How long had it been since she had been goofy? In another
corner an Arab painter, whose day job involved translations and oil man-
ifests, explained to a sympathetic cartoonist, who in his day job sold
things, why her paintings could not find a home in Beirut galleries. On
our deck, the size of a manhole cover, a writer stole a cigarette, peered
out at the twinkling lights and, if his faraway look could be trusted,
thought about something other than the emails waiting to be answered.

That the majority of people just like you and me, who only want
to write a little, draw a little, and drink some tea, must wake up every
morning and put on a false front is further proof that benevolent gods
do not exist. Could any but a sadistic god invent such lives for his best
and his brightest? Better to suppose that mindless cultural evolution,
producing a greater need for bankers than for poets, has caused all this
psychological pain and havoc. That is more theistic charity than athe-
ism; for what god would want to be associated with the murder of so
many artistic souls?

We had no string quartet playing. There was no fine champagne. There were no caterers and no staff circulating with smoked salmon. There were no party favors, no floral centerpiece, no ice sculpture. But there were lots of day jobs left at the door. And you know — you could throw such a party, too. How many of your co-workers are poets and mimes? How many writers in your town are posing as postal inspectors and real estate agents? Invite them over — not for a reading, not for a slide show, not for anything except the chance to let down their hair and laugh about stardust.

I think it is fair to say that the guest of honor, the out-of-town publisher, had a very good time. So good, in fact, that she moved her publishing company from Boston to San Francisco. She extrapolated from that evening that such theme parties were more likely to occur in San Francisco than anywhere else. Maybe she was rash; maybe she was right. I will do my small part in endorsing her choice by throwing her another shindig. In the not-too-distant future I will again invite over a bevy of artists who, in their own version of drag, dress up daily as investment bankers and nonprofit executives.

5.

SILENT RESPECT

I WOULD SEE HIM DRAWING IN PEN AND INK and colored pencils and sometimes writing in the same oversized sketchbook in which he drew. It seems to me that he wore a flannel shirt and jeans, though I also recall a colorful vest. I took him to be a visual artist, or maybe a children's book writer. He would sit at one table at the Owl and the Monkey, on Ninth Avenue in the Inner Sunset, and I would sit at another. Sometimes we sat across from one another, sometimes we sat at adjoining tables, and sometimes, when the café was very crowded, we even shared a table. But we never spoke, and we never acknowledged one another.

This went on for years. We saw each other everywhere. Sometimes our paths crossed in Golden Gate Park, whose entrance was just down the block from the café. He'd be out for his afternoon constitutional, and I'd be out for mine. We'd pass and continue not acknowledging one another, offering not even the slightest nod. Not to register even a glimmer of recognition when you recognize someone says volumes about the subtleties of human affairs. Who knew that eyes could hide so much?

It was very odd. We weren't shunning one another, since shunning implies animosity or a grudge. We weren't avoiding one another, dismissing one another — those aren't the right verbs. We were doing something very different. I believe that we were showing respect. By not acknowledging the other, we were saying something like the following: "I know that you spend your day in the world creating, that the world is your office and your home, just as it is mine, and since I wouldn't want you to barge into my office or home I will try assiduously not to barge into yours." I think that was what we were doing.

You might think that such mutual respect might have lead to conversations and some artistic bonhomie rather than to such studied avoidance. But it didn't — no more than it had for Dostoyevsky and Tolstoy, Picasso and Matisse, and many other fabled artistic peers. In the history of creating, there are friendships between peers, but then there is also some amazing distance-keeping, which can't be just attributed to envy, narcissism, or grandiosity. Such distance-keeping is doubtless a feature of alienation, self-protection, and the machinations of ego, but I am positive it is also a sign of respect. Picasso, who visited with Matisse only rarely, felt obliged to say upon Matisse's death, "Now I must paint for the both of us."

So many people who frequented the Owl in those years were absurdly happy producing very little. "I wrote two lines today — wow!" "I've gotten to the studio twice this week — I'm on a roll!" I knew in my heart that they weren't devoted to their craft, to their dreams, or to their freedom. They came to the café looking for beer, sex, and other amusements. Yes, they had a lot to say! — while, at the next table, my doppelgänger was actually working. He would draw; he would write; did that make him ridiculous? The others were having so much more fun! Was it absurd for him to work with dignity while the others were pairing off for the evening? I think not.

Recently a client pledged to write every day. After one day she emailed me her objections to her own pledge. "I see that I believe more in play," she explained. "I can't handcuff myself to the computer. Play is so important in life! Play is fundamental to the artist's personality. Play is the creative spirit. So I've decided to play more and not write until I am moved to write. I am really proud of myself for letting go of a commitment that was really just an albatross!" To which I mentally replied, "So Owl and the Monkey!"

At some point I began to see my doppelgänger on television, whenever an earthquake made the news. It turned out that he had written a bestseller on a famous earthquake and had become a talking head on the subject. What that meant to me was that I had been right all along: he had been real. He had been using the café as his study and not as a refuge from work. His celebrity status confirmed what I already knew, that his absorption in his colored pencils had not been for show. He had been deep in his fault lines, lost in his earthquake, making art.

On balance, it was probably smart of us not to speak. It is exactly because human beings can come to these unspoken arrangements that a café can serve as a writer's home. Without this — what shall we call it? — sanctifying of the café space and dignifying of the artist's profession, making each little round table a private studio, we would have to write, compose, and draw only at home. As if that wouldn't prove even more isolating! It may be alienating for two writers to maintain such a pointed, arch separation when they are separated by exactly two feet of café space, and still it makes good sense. It allows cafés to serve as temples for the religion of creativity.

Very often two writers will inhabit the same café for an hour and feel the urge to chat. They crave friendship, a reprieve from work, a little amusement, maybe even love. But the writer on this side, honoring the dignity of their mutual calling, will send the telepathic message to the writer on that side: "I see that you are working, and so am I." The other writer, without the slightest acknowledgment, will reluctantly agree and telepathically reply, "Yes." Each continues writing and foregoes interrupting the other. This is not the way that friendship blooms or that love arises, but it is the way that books get written.

6

KILLING LINES SOFTLY

I AM SITTING IN THE BACK GARDEN of Progressive Grounds, my home café at the corner of Cortland and Bennington in Bernal Heights, waiting for a client, soaking up the sun, and daydreaming. Just like that, sun-dappled and feeling quite special, a line arrives. It appears to be the opening line of a mystery novel starring a reporter-turned-detective. My antihero introduces himself as follows: "I needed to get deep into a story the way I needed to get deep into a woman."

I think I like the line. Or maybe I don't. But if it happens that I do, what then? What do you do with the opening line of a novel? Either you write the novel, or you discard the line. Aren't those a pair of amazing choices? Either you silence your pretty little line before it grows into an obsession, ruthlessly slitting its throat, or else you write the novel. The latter is surely a dramatic result of just innocently sitting in the sun for a moment. Dramatic and also wrenching, if you have other books lined up to write! So discarding your line as fast as you can looks like the logical imperative.

Are those the only choices, though, to let go of the line or to write the novel? Certainly not, since writers do a third thing all the time: they save their special line. They file it away. And isn't that sensible? Shouldn't lines be stored away like potatoes for the winter? Don't even Buddhists, who practice detachment, stock up on rutabagas and carrots? If even they can see the virtue of certain attachments, shouldn't we?

But it turns out that the Buddhist is psychologically acute when he preaches detachment. More often than not those good and bad fragments that we righteously accumulate bring us nothing but pain. Even worse, they cause paralysis. How many writers have been stymied by their accumulated words, words that, until attended to, prevent them from moving forward? Who doesn't have thirty-three thousand words of a novel sitting in some box or on some computer file that, merely by existing, badgers the writer and tires her out? What writer isn't burdened by — and saddened by — all those unprocessed ghosts?

Is the answer burning your inventory and starting fresh? How profligate and wasteful that seems! All those fragments! — some of them must be jewels. Indeed, just like you, I have gone to the basement and found some good words there. There are many fine words in our attics and basements. Yet and still, starting fresh is much the surer way to beauty. That being the case, why venture down to the basement at all when beauty can be found right there on the first floor?

Should we construct a rule, then, about never saving lines, about killing them off quickly or using them immediately, as if they had a shelf life of no more than a minute? No. There can be no such rule. There are lines worth saving, ideas worth saving, manuscripts worth saving. Saving is the way we accumulate intellectual capital, even if it is hard to make withdrawals. Not saving can't be the rule, any more than never rereading yesterday's output or never pouring through our journals for the seeds of a novel can be rules. On most days you will want to start fresh. On some days, however, you will have your good reasons for trudging down to the basement.

The answer, as usual, is that there is nothing but process. You kill off some lines, including, unfortunately, some great ones. You save some lines, including, unfortunately, some miserable ones. You start your collection of lines, chunks, fragments, journals, half-finished things, whole books that resemble books because they are sixty thousand words long and have a beginning, middle, and end but that aren't really books because they aren't any good yet. You accumulate. The longer you write, the more you accumulate. Like that of every writer, your space becomes haunted.

All those spared lines! You pledge to make some sense of that abundance, if it can be called that. But it makes you sick to think of rummaging there because, well, where exactly will you be? Not in some quaint, charming attic — no — but rather in a place of process, needing to choose from among a million saved words the words that, for some reason, you now decide matter. If you have the temerity to save words, you can be certain where you will end up one day. You will end up needing to choose among them and feeling anxious. How pleasant not saving seems, given that reality!

All things considered, I am happy to let my line go. No sexy mystery novel today. I send my line packing. Or so I would have sworn: but here it is again, showing up in this essay. How did it get here? Fancy that. I must have saved it.

I see my client. We have our session. I walk home. As I pass the market — not stopping for tuna sushi, though I want some — I wonder about an old novel from twenty years ago that I just had transcribed from paper to disk. How much of it is good? How much of it is bad? Do I have the stomach to look at it? Do I have the time? Would it be virtuous to rewrite it, a moral feather in my cap? Or would it be more like neurosis and vice? Well, at least it is now nicely saved to disk. Nicely saved! I hope you are laughing through your tears.

7.

A STREET LIKE HERB'S

I CAN'T REMEMBER THE EXACT HOUSE OR STREET. But it was somewhere in the San Francisco neighborhood of Laurel Village. The street sloped uphill from Sacramento Street toward Pacific Heights. Leafy trees shaded the quaint Edwardians and Victorians. Herb Wilner, my thesis advisor, was dying of cancer. Was I coming to his house because he was too ill to meet me at his office at San Francisco State, or did we routinely meet there? I can't remember.

I do remember that I lit up a cigarette as soon as I arrived. Herb asked me to put it out, because he was having trouble breathing. In those days I lit up wherever I liked, including in movie theaters. Herb whispered his request. He had always been soft-spoken, but now he had the added burden of illness.

It was another feature of my arrogance never to have considered reading his fiction. I think he had published one novel and one collection of short stories and that their setting was a New York City college, maybe even Brooklyn College, from which I flunked out in 1965. Without having read a single word, I'd concluded that I didn't respect the fiction of my professors. Since they were academics, they must be writing "academic fiction," something very different, I suspected, from the fiction of Dostoyevsky and Camus. So I couldn't be bothered.

He seemed like a sad man but not an embittered one. No doubt the illness accounted for the sadness. But there was something else, too, something about untapped potential and unrealized dreams. He told me a story that day about how he had accidentally missed a reviewer for the *New York Times.* His novel had just been published, and a *Times* reviewer, in possession of the novel but on the fence about reviewing it, had landed in San Francisco for the weekend. Spontaneously, the reviewer had phoned Herb to set up an interview. As the gods of whimsy would have it, Herb was out of town. The interview did not take place, nor did the review.

To have the *New York Times* not review your novel is one thing. That is terrible but at least not absurd. To have the *New York Times* not review your novel because you happened to be away for the weekend is both terrible and absurd. It makes you a little crazy and sad in a place that never heals. Herb recounted the story wistfully, as if it had been more a dream than nightmare. But to any writer listening, it had that nightmare quality.

I once knew a fellow in Fresno who ran a small publishing house. He published regional books about the West and the occasional odd something else. One book he published was the memoir of an actress who had spent a season on a hit television show of the seventies. The memoir was doing nicely and could already be counted a success, although, of course, its numbers did not compare to those of national bestsellers.

One Friday morning the publisher went off to a weekend book fair. So that he could concentrate on the fair and get a little break from the day-to-day challenges of hand-selling, he made the conscious decision not to check his phone messages while in Los Angeles. What, after all, were the chances of an important message coming in that Friday afternoon, Saturday, or Sunday? In fact, he had never gotten a book-related message so important that it couldn't wait a weekend.

Almost as soon as he drove off to Los Angeles, his office phone rang. One of Oprah's producers called and left a message. Was the actress available for a segment the following week? They wanted to feature her and the book. They were including three actresses from the seventies, and each would have a full twenty minutes of airtime. Since she was the only one with a book to sell, he had better get ready to publish another sizable printing, because he was about to have a national best-seller on his hands.

The publisher listened to the message when he got home Sunday night and dialed the Oprah producer that very instant, etiquette and the time difference be damned. She called him back on Monday. Ah, she said, they had moved on and picked someone else. Sorry. Good-bye. He made his best pitch for another chance — but no soap. That train had left the station.

There is the everyday pain that a writer experiences when she doesn't manage to write, writes drivel, or hears back from an editor rejecting her work. Then there is the occasional insane pain of an event that seems to have occurred only to mock you, that is proof of the existence of absurd, whimsical, malevolent gods who have targeted you as the object of their fun. How can you write for twenty years and miss the most important opportunity of your writing life because you took a well-earned weekend in the country? The only conclusion is that you are doomed.

So it seems, and so it feels. We must desperately fight the temptation to settle on that conclusion. We must enlist our "inner cognitive therapist" and reframe the matter, lancing the boil with logic, healing the wound with hope. We really don't dare let a thought like "Missing that reviewer is proof that my life is a farce" remain unchallenged. Designating your life a farce is a bigger tragedy than missing the *New York Times* book reviewer.

I never have reason to visit Laurel Village, and I rarely think of Herb Wilner anymore. But my mind has wandered his way today. I wish he'd been around that weekend to chat with the reviewer. I wish he'd had a nice *New York Times* review. And I hope that he's staked out a beautiful writing spot in heaven.

EARTHQUAKE COUNTRY

WE HAVE A SMALL BACKYARD, shared with our downstairs neighbor, that is microscopic by suburban standards but big enough for a table and chairs, a few sculptures, and San Francisco's favorite weeds. From the yard you access the basement, where the washer and dryer live. In the basement you get to see the old gal's foundation, which is sturdy with new cement in places but that has a nasty spot of old concrete mixed right from Bernal Hill in the months after the Great Quake. Take your fingernail to this hundred-year-old pebbly cement and it flakes right away. That is not a good thing in earthquake country.

It is proper that a stop on the bohemian international highway like San Francisco should exist on shaky ground. That San Francisco has known killer earthquakes and that it is always in the market for another great shake serve as excellent metaphors. Writers don't write books, after all, they let earthquakes pass through them. This is why describing a book to another person is such an exercise in communal folly. You are forced to say, "The book is about X." But what you would love to say, if the other person could understand you, is "I just gave birth during a cataclysm to this strange, darling thing." So, as metaphor, it is splendid that San Francisco is earthquake country.

The reality, however, is much less excellent, which is why we are paying attention to our foundation. The magnitude 8.25 quake that struck San Francisco on April 18, 1906, lasted forty-nine seconds. I invite you to watch the second hand on your clock as it ticks out forty-nine seconds. To call that an eternity, as your building is shaking, is an apt cliché. Twenty-eight thousand buildings were destroyed, two hundred and twenty-five thousand people were left homeless, six people were shot for looting, and one poor soul was shot by mistake. The earthquake was felt from southern Oregon to Los Angeles and as far inland as central Nevada.

Businessman Jerome Clark described what he saw as he disembarked from the commuter ferry that morning:

> In every direction from the ferry building flames were seething, and as I stood there, a five-story building half a block away fell with a crash, and the flames swept clear across Market Street and caught a new fireproof building recently erected. The

streets in places had sunk three or four feet, in others great humps had appeared four or five feet high. The street car tracks were bent and twisted out of shape. Electric wires lay in every direction. Wagons with horses hitched to them, drivers and all, lying on the streets, all dead, struck and killed by the falling bricks.

Jack London, a San Francisco reporter at the time of the Great Quake, described the quake's aftermath: "On Thursday morning, just twenty-four hours after the earthquake, I sat on the steps of a small residence on Nob Hill. All about me were the palaces of the nabob pioneers of Forty-nine. To the east and south, at right angles, were advancing two mighty walls of flames. I went inside with the owner of the house, who was cool, cheerful, and hospitable. 'Yesterday morning,' he said, 'I was worth six hundred thousand dollars. This morning this house is all I have left. It will go in fifteen minutes.'"

Writers live in perpetual earthquake country. You hope to gather your wits and work on your novel. The phone rings. It is your brother, telling you that your elderly mother is being mistreated and robbed by the nursing home where she resides. This crisis passes (it takes three months of your time). Again you try to gather your wits. You go into your day job as a professor of literature and learn that, rather than being able to teach the books you believe you should be teaching, this year you must teach assigned texts — horrible ones, to your mind. This crisis does not pass — all year you balk and feel sick to your stomach. Are your wits gathered? Not hardly.

Who isn't living in earthquake country, metaphorically speaking? But the writer is supposed to do her sensitive work even as the building shakes. How plausible is that? When your stomach is churning because your mate is angry at you for something or other, when you have a thousand things to attend to before dinner, how plausible is it that when dinner ends you'll be able to rush to your manuscript? In earthquake country — where we all reside — how are masterpieces even remotely possible?

Jack London wrote: "On Mission Street lay a dozen steers, in a neat row stretching across the street, just as they had been struck down by the flying ruins of the earthquake. The fire had passed through afterward and roasted them. All day Thursday and all day Friday the flames raged. Friday night saw the flames finally conquered, though not until Russian Hill and Telegraph Hill had been swept and three-quarters of a mile of wharves and docks had been licked up." I live a stone's throw from the ghosts of those charred steers and know that, whatever the tumult, I had better get on with my writing.

There is a special utility in living in a place where earthquakes are regularly on your mind. It helps you remember that the disturbances of everyday life must somehow be transcended. I think you'd have the same incentive to produce your own necessary calm if you lived in sight of Mount Vesuvius or on desert land previously inundated by the Great Flood. These reminders of cataclysm are helpful. It is good to recollect that everywhere is Earthquake Country; and that we write, if we write at all, not because a special silence has descended but because we have hushed the universe with our own fierce intention.

☙

FOR A YEAR I DATED A SCHIZOPHRENIC POET — let's call her Carol. Carol was ten years my senior, very sane, and very crazy. When insane, she had visions of roses appearing, threw a bowl of what she thought to be poisoned pumpkin soup at the counter girl at the Owl and the Monkey, and craved pastrami. When she was sane, she was a meditative vegetarian who lived on adzuki beans and classical music. Finally she got too crazy and got herself institutionalized in the locked ward of a local hospital. When she emerged, months later, she was still broken.

I loved Carol's poetry. I wish I could quote some of it here. I have an unpublished chapbook-length volume of her poetry in my possession, but I don't know how to contact her to get her permission. Probably she is dead. I presume that she is dead because, when insane, she lived much too dangerously. She would walk down the street poking people in the midriff. She would cross midblock, oblivious to traffic. She would shuffle (because of the Thorazine) into one scrape after another. Once I almost killed her myself. It is hard to imagine that she is still alive and kicking.

Very occasionally she would recite her poetry at an open-mike reading. This happened only rarely; like many writers, she was shy about performing and feared public humiliation. For every Dylan Thomas there are a thousand writers not quite equal to the task. It is no wonder that the typical book event feeds us so little, since the writer not only prays that he were elsewhere but also acts that way, preparing poorly, offering his audience crumbs, and counting the minutes until he can sign and be gone. Though Carol, too, came out rarely, when she did she gave the audience her whole heart.

People liked and responded to her poetry. But their expressions of appreciation rarely matched the depth of their admiration. They said mild things or things that didn't ring quite true. At the end of one reading, however, Carol got what every writer craves: the perfect validation. An older woman came up to her and said, "You are a real poet." This made Carol well up on the spot. It did not inoculate her from further bouts of madness but, as a true tonic, it probably postponed the onset of an episode by several months.

A writer can go her whole life without once being told, "You are a real writer." Just five words: Can a life be considered a failure, or significantly diminished, or an idiotic farce, simply by virtue of not having heard them? Yes, absurdly enough, it can. Every writer craves exactly that recognition, craves hearing exactly that mantra. It isn't that he needs flattery or adulation (though he may); it's a purer matter than that. He wants to write something worthy and have another person recognize its worthiness. How straightforward! It should be so easy to contrive — write a worthy thing and be told that it is worthy — but it isn't.

I went traveling with Carol to odd places — Disneyland, the Mount Baldy Zen Center, the Colorado River for white-water rafting. I have a photo of us on that raft, taken from a bridge, a souvenir supplied, for a nice price, by the rafting company. Carol looks beatific. I look like the mad one: wild beard, wild eyes, an unfiltered cigarette burning bright. Everyone is laughing and gleeful. No doubt it was a beautiful day and a beautiful setting; but my mind was elsewhere. At the end of the day Carol complained: "Couldn't you enjoy that? Did you have to smoke? I'm not sure I can be with you." But we stayed together until the madness returned and the hospitalization commenced.

I would visit her in the hospital. It was crazy-making in the extreme, playing basketball on the roof court with the inmates (who didn't have much game), trying to decipher Carol's coded messages, trying to fathom what to do with her reports of the constant rapes going on every night throughout the ward. She begged to be freed; she begged to be let off her antipsychotic medication; she incriminated everyone. No roses were appearing here. This was the lunatic asylum.

Now I take some slight comfort in that single validation. At least once Carol got to hear those crucial five words: "You are a real poet." Sometimes I pass her place on Stanyan Street, in San Francisco's Cole Valley, a place she could afford because her parents had money, a place where she spent her days slow-cooking beans, listening to late Beethoven, and writing poetry. She didn't work in the world; how could she? It is hard to work in the world when roses unexpectedly appear in your cubicle and the food in the canteen is poisoned. No; the world may be insane, but it nevertheless demands your sanity.

I remember the first time Carol told me that a rose had spontaneously materialized. It appeared on her hall floor, just outside her bedroom door. The sun was shining so brightly, streaming in through her bedroom window and pouring through the hall, that at first she hadn't seen the flower. Then she had; it was a perfect rose, blood red. I thought she was speaking metaphorically. I thought she was being a poet. I waited for her to smile and say, "Oh, I don't mean a real rose, of course! I mean —" But she was saying exactly what she meant.

We who write wait to hear those five words. Since they are hard to earn and hard to coax from an indifferent universe, they can prove devastatingly elusive. For many writers, they never arrive. Ah, Carol! At least you were rewarded once.

10.

CITY LIGHTS

THE PROBLEM WITH BOOKSTORES is all those books. I'm not analo-
gizing to a groaning buffet, to the idea that we writers are inclined to
buy three books every time we set foot into a bookstore, even though
we have twenty-nine unread ones at home. No, the problem with all
those books is that any one of them can precipitate a meaning crisis.

You are writing a book about herons and discover ten new books
about the bird. Damn! You are a Catholic and encounter a shelf-full of
books about priestly atrocities. Damn! You glance at the new novel

of an author you admire and find it deadly dull, which rings several bells, including the gong announcing that published authors can get away with second-rate work. Damn! You see that your excellent idea for a gift book has already been used. Damn! An avowed evolutionist, you peek into a book on intelligent design and find it riveting. Thunder and damnation!

The answer isn't to avoid bookstores and books. The answer is to understand how sneakily meaning crises arise in the course of everyday living. Meaning is not set; it is in turbulent flux. It is impossible to maintain constant meaning, as if you were a rock, without acting like a rock, without foregoing thought and learning nothing from experience. If the choice is to maintain a rock-solid grip on meaning by staying inert or to proceed like a high-wire artist, trembling in the wind a thousand feet above meaninglessness, which will it be?

If you opt for the risk, then bookstores are back in the picture. Yes, they are dangerous places; but you have opted for danger! Yes, a book you encounter may explode your worldview; but you have allowed for that possibility and carry around, as a first aid kit, your wry love of the human condition. In fact, you are not only the recipient of meaning crises; you are also a meaning provocateur. Bookstores may be battlefields, but they are also the places where new meaning gets made, including the meaning bound up in the books you write.

Now that you have allowed bookstores back into your life, you will want to visit that San Francisco landmark, City Lights Bookstore in North Beach. It is an institution, as is Vesuvio Café, next door, and the Tosca Café Bar, across Columbus Avenue. Alas, the tour buses no longer stop at City Lights to provide visitors with a glimpse of Beatniks. But it remains the right place to honor the fiftieth anniversary of Allen Ginsberg's *Howl* and the only place to view the Zapatista Mural, next door in Jack Kerouac Alley.

This corner of Columbus and Broadway, where City Lights has lived for fifty years, doesn't feel a bit like Paris. Yet City Lights is a sure nexus between Paris and San Francisco. Literary historian Bill Morgan described this revered landmark in *The Beat Generation in San Francisco*:

[Painter and poet Lawrence] Ferlinghetti loved the idea of a bookstore since his good friend George Whitman in Paris had started one called Librairie Mistral (later renamed Shakespeare & Co). The little one-room, pie-shaped bookstore opened in June 1953 and Martin and Ferlinghetti began selling new quality paperbacks and early alternative newspapers and magazines. Out front on the sidewalk there were used books in Parisian-style bookracks with lids that could be closed at night (like quayside kiosks in Paris)...

From his graduate-school days at the Sorbonne in Paris, Ferlinghetti was familiar with the tradition of booksellers also being publishers, and he wanted to print small editions of poetry in paperback format. City Lights' first publication was his own collection, *Pictures of the Gone World*, published in 1955.... This was number one of the Pocket Poets Series, inspired by a French publisher's Poets of Today series.

As a San Francisco-Paris nexus, it is the ideal place to lose your meaning bearings, just as you might in a Sorbonne classroom. It is also the very place to recover those bearings. You can make the entire round-trip in a single afternoon, wandering in and finding, in a book on noir cinema or a volume of Baudelaire (both published by City Lights), some phrase that turns your world concave. You reel at the meaning leak (that feels like spinal fluid escaping), quickly regroup because you

are existentially adept, and celebrate your survival with a beer at Vesuvio's or a cappuccino at Tosca's. What an afternoon! Perfect for a writer.

You can have the same disorienting adventure in any quadrant of
the city. Find a book that shakes your world at Red Hill Books in Bernal
Heights; celebrate your survival across the street at Progressive Grounds
Café. If you're in the Haight, make it the Booksmith and Rockin' Java.
The Richmond? Green Apple and Java Source. Downtown? Stacey's
and a Starbuck's. But the classic place to lose and find meaning is at
City Lights, that venerable Beat haunt on Columbus.

It is a place to pay your respects. Remember that in 1956 Ferlinghetti first published Ginsberg's *Howl and Other Poems*, defended it
against obscenity charges in a high-profile trial, prevailed, and went on
to sell a million copies of it in its City Lights edition. It became one of
the great sellers in the history of poetry. That is a lot to consider and be
thankful for. In *The Fall of America*, Allen Ginsberg described City
Lights as "home." It is your home, too.

AT THE CHAISE LOUNGE

THE CHAISE LOUNGE IS A NEIGHBORHOOD BAR and woman's bar on Cortland Street. It is where Ann and I go to unwind. We used to go to the Wild Side West, similarly lesbian oriented, but then the Chaise Lounge opened, and we switched allegiance. They pour a very nice Coppola Merlot, sometimes they have pretzels (so as not to be disappointed, we bring our own), and they play Blondie and the B-52s on the sound system. It is our second home just down the block.

For the lady carpenters out to impress their femme dates, they have an amusement park game where for a quarter you can test your grip. (Hint: if you yank the machine toward you as you grip the handle, it gives a much higher reading.) The lighting is subdued and classy, the banquettes are comfy, the bartenders are friendly, and the house dog is placid. Sometimes they even put out peanuts.

As I sip my good Merlot I am reminded of another San Francisco-Paris nexus, similar to the psychic ties between City Lights Bookstore and Shakespeare & Company. That nexus is embodied in a single female, Alice B. Toklas. Partner of the Paris-based writer and salon-keeper Gertrude Stein (the two were probably the most famous lesbian couple ever), described as "a chain smoker with a slight mustache, given to exotic dress, Gypsy earrings and manicured nails," Alice was, before setting off for Paris in 1907, the quintessential San Franciscan: Jewish, lesbian, and musical.

In her autobiography, *What Is Remembered*, Alice wrote:

Soon after we returned to San Francisco [from Europe], I was sent to Miss Mary West's school. A little girl in my class asked me if my father was a millionaire. I said I did not know. Had we a yacht? she continued. When she learned that we hadn't, she lost interest. My mother said it was time to send me to another school where the little girls would be less snobbish. The new school, Miss Lake's, was a gay happy one. At once I formed a close friendship with a radiant, resilient, brilliant little girl, Clare Moore, which was to last until her death only a few years ago.

Her mother perhaps did not switch Alice's school quickly enough. Or maybe there were just too many servants running baths and setting tables in Alice's childhood. Or maybe she was born with a fascist gene.

For whatever reasons of nature or nurture, Alice ran as far to the political right as royalty. It would be nice if I could report that she and
Gertrude, both of whom ought to have understood the extraordinary
preciousness of freedom, had championed it. Unfortunately, they didn't.
They backed the Nazis.

Gertrude supported Franco in the Spanish Civil War and translated
the speeches of Vichy leader Marshal Pétain into English. During
World War II, she and Alice retired to a country home in Ain, where
they escaped persecution because of their friendship with the gay col-
laborator Bernard Fay. When, after the War, Fay was sentenced to a life-
time of hard labor, they energetically campaigned for his release. Later,
Alice contributed money to his prison break. All this makes one wonder — even about the art they championed, all those Picassos and
Braques on the walls of 27, rue de Fleurus.

It is sobering but not surprising that Alice and Gertrude should
have chosen fascism. In every group, gay or straight, rich or poor, musical or tone-deaf, there are lordly tyrants. Since this tyranny can come
from anywhere, including from the lady on the next bar stool, vigilance
is necessary. You can't judge a person by what he or she shares with you,
whether it is skin color, religious affiliation, or sexual orientation. You
can't give people a pass because looking at them is like looking in the
mirror. They must earn your allegiance.

Your freedom is not guaranteed. It is always at risk — always.
Throughout history, almost as if they have studied the same book,
tyrants have rounded up the Jews, the gypsies, and the homosexuals as
their first official act. Alice was all three and ought to have known better. That she could send Gertrude such sweet love notes and miss the
boat on freedom is one of life's painful mysteries. You desperately want
them to be democrats, these two; but they weren't.

In the world of Stein scholarship, the depth and meaning of her pro-Vichy, pro-fascist positions are debated. Some excoriate her; others exonerate her. Some make nothing of her Roman emperor's haircut; others point to it as emblematic. Some make the case that the depth of her love for Alice proves something; others point out that plenty of Nazis loved their partners, dogs, and children. I don't know the truth of the matter; but from this far distance I'm afraid that she looks to have been fully in bed with other literati of the era like Pound the Nazi and Elliot the anti-Semite.

I don't know the truth about Gertrude and Alice. What I do know is that being a writer is not a badge of honor unless you wear it honorably. The ability to make fine sentences is not in and of itself praiseworthy. That ability is merely a feature of some skill, some intellect, and maybe an eye for beauty. Full-blown fascists have written excellently, just as they have proven to be great orators and, like Nero, good amateur musicians. No, fine writing isn't enough to get you a nod. There must be goodness tossed in. Otherwise you are a mere artist and not a humanist.

This calls for a second Merlot. The bar scene is heating up. Conversations are growing more animated. Mint leaves are bruised for one Mojito after another. We share our bag of pretzels with the four women to our right. We like to buy a very big bag, expressly for sharing. Having shared, we sit back and silently compliment the vintner. If you have a bar in your town like the Chaise Lounge, where women can come and go without fear or interference, protect it.

12.

DEMOGRAPHICS

WHY IS SAN FRANCISCO A LEGENDARY WRITERS' TOWN and still a
writing hotbed, so hot that our annual LitQuake event finds hundreds
of writers reading in the bars and cafés along Valencia? Two great nearby
colleges, Berkeley and Stanford, have something to do with it. It is rare
to find a world-class public university like Berkeley, regularly ranked as
the world's finest public college, and a world-class private university like
Stanford in the same vicinity. Between them, they concentrate a lot of
smart people in a small geographic area. Smart people are interesting
and have ideas. They invent things like Silicon Valley, they like to read

and write (although thirteenth in U.S. population, San Francisco is third in book buying), and they are more likely to call God a she, if they invoke gods at all.

San Francisco is ranked second nationally in the education level of its workforce. (Washington, D.C., ranks first, which is obviously an artifact of the presence of big government.) Smart, educated people fill our businesses. Folks with odd advanced degrees in urban planning, ethnomusicology, and Eastern studies work in companies they would like to dismantle. They dream of building new cities, playing bluegrass music, and bringing mindfulness into the twenty-first century. This passionate, educated, eclectic, dreamy, hardworking, half-disillusioned, half-manic brain trust wanders this hilly town and, like the fog, seeps into its bistros, its Mystery Bookstore, its leather bars, everywhere.

And they keep bumping into one another. San Francisco is physically a tiny town. New York City is 303 square miles in size, Los Angeles 469, Chicago 227, Houston 579, Phoenix 474. San Francisco, by contrast, is a mere 46.7. It is smaller than all other great American cities except Boston, which is only 48 square miles in size. Smart people with ideas are crammed together and stand in line at the same cafés, go to the same outdoor film festivals (Bernal Heights has enough filmmakers to support its own outdoor festival, with films shown in schoolyards and atop Bernal Hill), shop at the same farmers' markets, and frequent the same bars.

Probably half the city passes through a bustling Chez Maman, the tiny French bistro down the block on Cortland where we go for steak and fries. (The first time we dined there our waiter tried to take away my Dubonnet, although it had a full sip left. I cried, "Wait! There's something left." He replied, "Are you French?") This shoulder-to-shoulder acquaintanceship, moderated by complete anonymity, allows you to feel bathed in communal thought without being bothered by actual contact. It is virtually the exact opposite of small-town America, where all you know is everybody's business.

Then there are the Jews. As a home for Jews, the San Francisco Bay Area (which includes Berkeley, Marin, and other points north, south, and east) ranks seventh among all the cities of the Diaspora (after New York, Los Angeles, Paris, Philadelphia, Chicago, and Boston). According to the World Jewish Congress, more than two hundred thousand Jews live in the Bay Area. This means that the things that Jews bring, among them smarts and culture, help make this a smart, cultured place. You wouldn't know it by the delis, but you would by the zeitgeist.

Then there are the Chinese. San Francisco is 30 percent Asian, the largest Asian population in America outside Hawaii. It is 20 percent Chinese; there are more Chinese in San Francisco than in any other American city. The Chinese population in San Francisco has grown by 85 percent in the past twenty-five years. Whole bowling teams are Chinese, whole ballroom dance classes are Chinese, whole gambling buses to the Indian casinos are filled with Chinese. Like the Jews, they honor education and those icons of education, books.

Then there are the Latinos. San Francisco is 15 percent Latino and Hispanic, the majority ensconced in the Mission District. Mariachi bands fill the restaurants of the Mission every Friday and Saturday night, families dress for church, and schoolchildren go on outings to see the Mission's murals. It warms a writer's heart to find, all in a row, a Chilean restaurant, an El Salvadoran restaurant, a Brazilian restaurant, a wired café with red walls and a sea of laptops, an Ecuadorian restaurant, and so on.

Then there are the gays. Gay towns are creative towns, and gay, creative towns attract the next generation of queers who go on to write books, make movies, dance, and hold hands. It's estimated that between 10 and 20 percent of San Francisco's population is gay. This means that there are between seventy-five thousand and one hundred and fifty thousand pro-art, pro-music, pro-book radical outsiders who define whole neighborhoods of the city. The Castro is as gay as the Mission is Latin and the Richmond Chinese.

Then there are the Italians, the founders of old North Beach and the fishermen of these Pacific waters. They came from the coastal fishing villages along the gulf of Genova and the Ligurian Sea and found the fishing here to be good. By 1870 they were providing 90 percent of the fish San Franciscans were devouring. Their North Beach cafés provided sanctuary and cover for Allen Ginsburg, William S. Burroughs, Jack Kerouac, Ken Kesey, ruth weiss, and the other Beats, hippies, and outlaws, all fleeing McCarthy's America.

Then there are the other constituencies, the African American 8 percent, the Irish 8 percent, the German 8 percent, the English 6 percent. Taken all together, the modal San Franciscan is a half-Chinese, half-Latin, half-gay, quarter-Italian, quarter-Jewish, quarter-Irish college-educated, opinionated, compassionate, liberal, book-buying, bar-hopping, gallery-going closeted or out writer looking for a literary agent and a good Merlot. This is not Orange County, and writers want to live here.

The Free Speech Movement and the Summer of Love were manifestations of radical good sense caused not by ocean breezes and the ringing of cable car bells. They didn't arise because San Francisco has a fine outlook and natural beauty. They were the fruit of the little democratic energy America has left to offer, embodied in a few hundred thousand San Franciscans and their Bay Area cohorts who feel the Bill of Rights in their bones. They arose here because like-minded people were drawn here. This is one of the places you come to be with smart people who know the difference between a café and a mall — and know which they prefer.

ONE WINTER EVENING I find myself in the green room of the beautiful new theater on the campus of the North Carolina School of the Arts, waiting to give a creativity chat to a crowd of a few hundred Carolinians. I'd given this chat many times before, varying the title to suit the audience but presenting essentially the same material, and can now deliver it on a dime, starting up the instant they say "Go!" and ending directly on the hour. In fact, when I delivered this chat to a group of Indiana arts administrators, what impressed the conference chair the most, more than the chat's content, was the fact that I ended so promptly — perhaps a little left-handed praise, wouldn't you say?

Nowadays I deliver my chat without any notes, although I keep a sheet handy with seven headlines in case I blank out. This is a far cry from my early days of speaking in support of my books. In 1992 I gave my first book talk at the Green Apple, an independent bookstore in the Richmond District of San Francisco, on the corner of a street of Chinese vegetable markets and Russian bakeries. I had no clue what I was doing. It wasn't that I hadn't prepared — no, indeed — but what I'd prepared was wondrously odd and constituted the strangest chat that any audience has ever had to suffer through.

Instead of describing *Staying Sane in the Arts*, the book I was hawking, or, simpler yet, reading from it (as most writers on tour do), I prepared a cross between a stump speech and an academic white paper on something I called "The Artist Corps." I think I meant the speech to be a visionary call to arms on the order of "I have a dream . . . for artists." It might have fit the bill if I'd been delivering it on the Washington Mall to a crowd of a million marching artists. To this small crowd, drifting in off Clement Street after shopping for sugar snap peas and piroshki, it was a bore and a monstrosity. To seal their fate and further make them wish that they had chosen the comedy club across the street, I read the darn thing, slowly (to give it weight) and softly (because I always speak softly).

No one left as I spoke — perhaps because they had nodded off. No one cheered when I finished. No one had any questions. My literary agent at that time, Linda Allen, who had come to support me, couldn't find a way, despite her many social graces, to compliment me. So I wandered home alone — but not crestfallen. What went through my mind was the following question: "I wonder what would work better?" It took me a while — some years — to figure that "better" out, but I knew to retire that Artists Corps speech and never to dust it off again.

There are four paths in life for the public performer. One is Mozart's: you do things perfectly at the age of six and continue perfectly until your last breath. That's the path of say, oh, one in a billion. Then there's the path of not trying, of having no interest or too much fear. That's the path of most everyone. In the middle are the folks who perform and do not get better and the folks who perform and do get better.

During one six-month period in the early 1960s Bob Dylan made some truly incredible strides. His guitar playing improved by a quantum leap, his new songs soared, even his voice, which you wouldn't think could improve dramatically, did. At the beginning of that year he was ordinary; by mid-year he was extraordinary. Not a single soul saw the change coming, but come it did.

I, too, improved. The distance between the Green Apple chat and the North Carolina School of the Arts chat was more than a dozen years and three thousand miles. It was that nonlinear distance known as a learning curve. I had learned how to speak in public. This is very important news for your writing life, since you may be preventing yourself from writing out of fear that you won't do an adequate job of supporting your books when they appear. Maybe you won't — *the first time*. So what?

The specter of speaking to an audience about their books frightens many writers. It can frighten them seriously enough that they don't write the book. This fear is based on a fundamental confusion: that there is some reason why they should be expected to do a good job of public speaking on their first attempt. There is no good reason. They should be expected to do goofy things like present a manifesto on the Artists Corps, read with their head down, be inaudible and quaking, or in some other way fail to mesmerize their audience. In short, they should be expected to make a fine mess right out the gate.

If you were at the Green Apple that evening in 1992, I pity you. I know that you would never have guessed that the stiff, boring fellow reading his speech would one day approach oratory. Fooled you! As a writer supporting your own books, you can perform the same magic trick. You can appear one year in support of your first book and make a riotous hash of your chats and your interviews. Then, two years later, having learned a ton, you can appear in support of your second book and look like Kennedy in Berlin. The task is not to get it right the first time. The tasks are to learn from your pratfalls, and, by learning, to improve.

TOURIST DESTINATION

IF YOU LIKE TO WRITE OUTDOORS and you visit San Francisco, I imagine you'll pick a spot in Golden Gate Park, maybe in front of the Conservatory of Flowers, or someplace along the Embarcadero, maybe beside the Anchor, or on a bench in Washington Square Park, in North Beach, or maybe on the grass of the Marina Green, either toward the Fort Mason end or down under the Golden Gate Bridge. There are plenty of other choices, too, depending, for instance, on whether you want to catch a glimpse of Latino children playing, ducks bobbing for stale bread, or gay men sunbathing. A writer visiting or living in San Francisco has plenty of options for outdoor writing.

Here is one option, odd because it's a tourist spot — which is why I've chosen it. San Francisco's billion-dollar tourist industry is important to the city, just as the tourist dollars that pour into Paris, London, or Rome are. But the real importance of tourists, to you as a writer, is why they have chosen to leave their hometowns and travel. It's easy enough to scorn them, to feel superior, to laugh at their purchases and their proclivities. It is hardly a stretch to see their forlorn vacations as an indictment of our lowbrow culture. A little compassion, please. They are traveling because their hearts are breaking.

Tourists come to cities like San Francisco for reasons that run deeper than "there are things to do there," since the things they end up doing, like riding a cable car or traipsing through an anchored submarine — mind your head, please! — are not that special. You wouldn't spend three thousand dollars to fly you, the wife, and the kids to see if a certain bridge is really golden (it isn't — it's red-orange). No, cities like San Francisco are important because the heart needs a break from its everyday aching. That's the only reason tourism exists. Virtually nobody is traveling three thousand miles to visit a museum.

An everyday aching heart needs many things. It needs an ocean, San Francisco's Pacific or New York's Atlantic, or at least a good river, like the Thames, the Seine, the Danube, the Arno. The heart needs an artist on a stool, drawing caricatures, like you get in Montmartre or along that stretch of Fisherman's Wharf that fronts Ghirardelli Square, known as Aquatic Park, where I am sending you today. The heart needs a reason to stand quietly in a line, beating and not needing to think, feeling a sea breeze and foregoing its usual miseries. The line that you get to watch, as you enjoy the privilege of writing in Aquatic Park, is the line of folks waiting to board the cable car at the Hyde Street Cable Car Turnaround.

An aching heart needs an ice cream cone in a new location, a change of flavors, a choice of picture postcards to send to loved ones to whom it never says "I love you" except when it is on vacation. The heart needs an oddity or two, something to make it smile, like the arctic swimmers, members of the Dolphin Club and looking like penguins, who toddle into the freezing Bay at this location. The heart needs the Municipal Pier, jutting out at the foot of the park, with its Vietnamese fishermen and views of Alcatraz Island. The heart needs the cultivated flowers, the benches, the footpaths: it needs exactly what this spot has to offer.

Yes, Aquatic Park is a tourist destination; because what the tourist's heart needs resides here. It is what any heart needs, really. Colorful kitsch, Irish coffees, kites in the air, saltwater taffy, shrimp cocktail in a Dixie cup, foghorns, and hawkers. You do need a pseudo-African shawl or a rainbow-painted plate for a light switch, but you do not need to be thinking about your niece who died young or the mess you made of your first marriage. The shawls and the switch plates are blessedly distracting. Not thinking, for a few hours, is the blessing.

An aching heart also needs its legends. Here, sitting in front of Ghirardelli Square, you can conjure Domenico Ghirardelli, born in Rapallo in 1817, who left Italy to set up chocolate shops in Uruguay and Peru. There he met the Californian James Lick, who was making his fortune in South America and who brought back six hundred pounds of Domenico's chocolate to San Francisco. Lured by Lick and the blandishments of the Gold Rush, Domenico arrived in California in 1848, made his chocolates, prospered, and opened the Europa Hotel, only to see it burn to the ground in the Great Fire of 1851. Four days later, his heart still aching, he saw his other properties, in Stockton, California, burn to the ground in an unrelated fire.

An aching heart is likewise soothed by nautical dreaming. What wounded heart doesn't require tramp steamers, desert islands, hidden treasure? Aquatic Park sits at the foot of Ghirardelli Square and oversees a small, historic fleet of vessels: the 1886 square-rigger *Balclutha*, the 1895 schooner *C. A. Thayer*, the 1890 steam ferryboat *Eureka*, the 1891 scow schooner *Alma*, the 1907 steam tug *Hercules*, the 1914 paddlewheel tug *Eppleton Hall*. If this isn't enough to conjure with, just consider: the *Balclutha*, finding itself in Polynesia one year, got to appear in *Mutiny on the Bounty*. Doesn't that bring Charles Laughton directly to mind? Aren't you smiling just a little?

Come and sit among the tourists. They have good reason to be here, therapeutic reasons, and so do you. Pick a comfy spot. Enjoy the colorful scene. Write. In the space of an hour, hundreds of tourists will have come and gone. When they get back home, they will gush about the gorgeousness of Ghirardelli Square, the lusciousness of its chocolate, and the artiness of the scene — meaning you. You, sitting there writing, are what the tourist needs. You gladden the heart. You, writing and living the dream, are a sight for a sore heart.

15.

EGG-CETERA

I OFTEN DO THE ODD THING of having folks in my online trainings start out their lesson responses with the following affirmation: "My creative work and my creative life matter to me." I might have them do this for a month running, and, if they agree to make this announcement, it is almost impossible for them not to turn their creative life around. You try to say thirty consecutive times that you and your work matter (even if you don't believe it), and see if you don't change for the better.

On some days I may sit at my computer from six A.M. until eight
P.M. reading and answering the emails that these trainings generate. I
often have several trainings going — one for creativity coaches, one for
writers, one for visual artists, one for performers. The world has never
seen anything quite like it, me sending out a particular creativity exercise, and getting writers in Corsica, Australia, Omaha, and other points
on the globe to crack an egg as a prelude to writing.

I could be anywhere, watching the sun rise, typing my first emails
of the day. But because San Francisco is a place where an annual Arab
film festival and an annual Jewish film festival can co-exist nicely, at a
time when our country is led by seriocomic characters out of a play by
Dante and Molière, it is appropriate that this worldwide support system should emanate from this particular city. But of course you aren't
listening — isn't your mind still on that last paragraph, wondering
about that egg?

Why do I have my coaches and artists crack an egg? Writers find it
enormously difficult to do the thing that in the abstract sounds pretty
easy: write and keep writing. You might write twenty novels in ten years
if you happened to write two pages a day. But no one writes twenty
novels in ten years except the occasional romance writer. It is much
more common for a writer to write a draft of a first novel and half a
draft of a second in those ten years — and feel horrible about her output. Why is she writing so little?

When we're lost in the trance of writing, it takes hardly an hour to
write two pages. Isn't it amazing that it should prove so hard to entertain
that single hour of daily work? What could possibly be going on? An egg
provides the complete answer. If you want to crack an egg because you
are baking a cake, you simply whack it (carefully) on the side of your
bowl, break it, and drop its contents into the bowl. Nothing simpler. But

if you are just sitting around thinking about baking a cake and worrying that your cake will stink, that egg becomes a strange fortress.

There is something almost scary about cracking an egg when we aren't ready to use it, something that makes us squeamish, something traumatizing about breaking that shell and exposing its yellowness. Every day, an encounter like that stands between us and our writing. We need to crack through our resistance and expose our slimy word choices and our sticky paragraphs. If we are doing well, no problem, we crack on through. But if we doubt our writing even just a little, a hard shell arises to protect us from what we fear will be a miserable encounter. If we are to have that encounter, there is nothing to be done but to shatter that shell with a sledgehammer.

Would-be writers prefer to live uncomfortably in their shell of resistance rather than risk cracking it and exposing their insufficiencies. You may be reminded of Gregor Samsa in Kafka's *The Metamorphosis.* Gregor awakes one morning to discover that he has become a cockroach. Tellingly, Gregor doesn't mind the transformation all that much. Yes, it is absurd, bewildering, and inconvenient but, on balance, no big deal. His reaction is odd, to say the least, unless we get the metaphor.

We see in Gregor's attitude exactly that of the writer manqué. It is the attitude of the would-be artist who has not accepted that he must crack through his shell every day, that he must prove himself every day, that he must free himself every day — or else remain unfree. Gregor is a willing cockroach. You can be certain that he would see little reason to crack through his resistance and make art, if art-making was his dream, just as he can see little reason to resent his awful transformation and take a hammer to his cockroach shell.

Make the point of this lesson real by doing the following. Get a carton of jumbo eggs and put it in your refrigerator. Place a bowl beside your computer, preferably a very small bowl that will hardly hold the contents of one egg (so as to risk making a fine mess). Begin your daily writing session by cracking an egg into that bowl, dropping in the oozy insides and the shell fragments. Then write.

Experience the cracking of that egg as the cracking through of your resistance. Feel yourself exhale as you crack it, as if you had just survived something dangerous. You have. You have become a free man or woman. You have crossed to the other side. You are now free to write well, or to write poorly. This is what you must do every day. If you prefer not to waste eggs, then perform this daily joust just with courage.

These are the sorts of things I chat about with the coaches, writers, visual artists, and performers in my trainings. I sit in Bernal Heights, my cup of coffee beside me, and they sit in Berlin, Tampa, or Seattle, their cup of coffee, egg bowl, and egg at the ready. I can almost hear the blessed cracking from here. As often as not, by cracking that egg they are able to resume their novel or their collection of sonnets after two years or ten years of not trying. You, too, may want to get cracking.

16.

WEST PORTAL FIXTURE

MY MOTHER IS NINETY-SIX and lives on West Portal Avenue, west of Twin Peaks and a long stone's throw from the ocean. West Portal is a bustling thoroughfare with trolleys running down the center and throngs of shoppers from the good neighborhoods to the west and the even better neighborhoods to the east. She has lived on West Portal for thirty-five years, since retiring from her Brooklyn clerical job. Because of West Portal's endless parade of life, she calls it heaven.

With her teeth out, she looks even older than ninety-six. Everywhere in her messy apartment are scraps of paper upon which she has recorded her thoughts. Every room has pads at the ready in case she should have a new idea. Nearing ninety-seven, she still feels compelled to get her thoughts down, about gay marriage, stem cell research, and the missing link, to name three of her current favorites. Her ideas about science are a little naive and loony; she spent one day recently toying with the possibility that gophers were the missing link. But she had a great day conjuring.

She lives in a roomy apartment for which she pays one-fifth the market rate. She pays three hundred dollars a month because she has lived there so long and because the building's owners have been generous. Every few years her rent goes up five or ten dollars. To be sure, they haven't painted or done a stitch of work on the apartment in those thirty-five years — in keeping with her express wishes, since she hasn't wanted to be bothered. So the paint is peeling in long ribbons, and her stove is an incredible burnt sienna. But its color does not prevent her from cooking endless small meals all day long, in an assortment of cookware that no one has seen since the Bronze Age.

It is no coincidence that she writes all day and that she lives independently. These facts are both manifestations of her curiosity, her love of life, and her fierceness. They flow from the same well of iconoclasm. She hasn't owned a television set in decades, nor has she wanted one. No time for television, she says, between the shopping, cooking, and writing. She still hops the bus to travel halfway across the city to support a certain market where they stock eggs by the half-carton. It appears that grocers on West Portal will only sell eggs by the dozen — an absurdity, she contends, since what can a single person do with a dozen eggs?

She wears rags, but of the most interesting and colorful sort, maybe a quilted vest in clown colors over a cashmere sweater found at the Good Will over a comfy shirt that was new during the New Deal. People do not know what to make of her and figure she's a street person. If she sits down with her cup of coffee on the bench in front of the bagel shop, someone is sure to want to drop a five-dollar bill into her cup, annoying her mightily. When she throws out the garbage in the can in the alley between her building and the Italian restaurant, a young fellow who only speaks Italian will rush out from the restaurant kitchen to present her with old bread and tired potatoes. People aren't quite sure if she is destitute, but they feel like erring on the side of magnanimity.

We have lovely chats, although they are actually monologues. I am reader to her writer; she speaks her unwritten books. She will tell me in her sardonic way that she is still having trouble with the algebraic concept of slope. She is not asking me to explain it, which she knows I could. Rather, she is using slope as an introduction to a subject she's been pondering, the multiple meanings of *incline*. Have I thought much about the word *incline*, she asks, or about *inclination*? She pulls out her pad to refresh her memory. After a bit, having expertly deconstructed inclination, she is on to disinclination.

I saw her today, and her first word was haberdashery. After a bit she switched the subject. "What does the word *affair* mean to you?" I gave her my answer, which she didn't hear. No matter. "Last night I had a dream that incorporated two meanings of the word *affair*," she continued. "I was a bridesmaid at a wedding — meaning one. One of the guests at the wedding was a man from my office who had a quiet charisma and who interested me. He would take his lunch break with my girlfriend and me. But we never saw each other outside of work. Meaning two, so to speak. Because I couldn't seem to get dressed properly for the wedding

— I had only rags to wear, and the bride complained — and also because that fellow was there, I found myself saying to the bride, 'This is a poor affair.' After that I had a Christmas dream in the most beautiful colors."

She grew up in Manhattan, on East Seventieth Street between Avenue A and First Avenue, and went to the library daily. She loved books and read voraciously. Her secret desire was to become a librarian. Even more secret, so secret that she has not yet recognized it, was the desire to write. She has been writing for the last thirty years, every day, in her manner. No books have coalesced. The scraps wander about the apartment, as if alive, and eventually find their way into the garbage. Hardly any scrap contains even a full sentence. Words; fragments; are these enough to anoint a person a writer? If you were a woman born in 1909 into the lower classes? Yes, I think so. Absolutely.

As you read this, Esther may have passed on. Or she may still be writing. Or, of course, both.

This straggling town shall be a vast metropolis. Has any other city a future like San Francisco?

— MARK TWAIN

I think San Francisco is the best place in the whole world for an easy life.

— IMOGEN CUNNINGHAM

San Francisco is incredibly beautiful, all hills and bridges and blinding blue sky and boats and the Pacific Ocean. I am madly unhappy but I love it here.

— DYLAN THOMAS

It is an odd thing, but everyone who disappears is said to be seen in San Francisco. It must be a delightful city, and possess all the attractions of the next world.

— OSCAR WILDE

17.

THE PERFECT LANDLORD

POP DEMAREST, A SAN FRANCISCO CHARACTER, who no doubt was mad, in the good sense, owned some Russian Hill cottages that he rented out on the cheap to writers and artists. By all accounts Demarest was the perfect landlord, charging little, spending his evenings lubricated and dancing naked outdoors to the accompaniment of tinny gramophone music, and often forgetting to collect the rent. What more could you want from your landlord?

His grateful tenants included the photographer Dorothea Lange, her husband, the painter Maynard Dixon, and any number of writers, among them Frank Norris and Ambrose Bierce. Perfect for writers, this arrangement was apparently perfect for Pop, too. He lived to be eighty-seven, a long life in those days. It was an amazingly long life, really, when you consider that he lived not in, but under, one of his cottages, in a cistern pipe with eighteen cats.

Contrast the beauty of a cottage of your own, administered by a blitzed, benign landlord, a cottage where you can live anonymously and write naturally, to incarceration in something like the Handy Writers' Colony, located a long time ago in rural Illinois. It was there that James Jones, about-to-be-author of *From Here to Eternity* but then a young AWOL soldier just out of the hospital, got "nurtured" by one Lowney Handy, a mad-in-the-bad-sense failed writer.

In her review of *James Jones and the Handy Writers' Colony*, Andrea Lynn described Lowney's nurturing methods:

At the Handy Colony, Lowney (rhymes with phony) Handy was the chief cauldron stirrer. Homophobic, charismatic, nurturing and neurotic, she was a fan of Eastern religions and the Spartan lifestyle. To break her students psychologically, she banned liquor, sex, and unauthorized food. Her temper tantrums were legendary. She even attacked people, including Jones' wife, with a knife.

Handy also adopted unorthodox teaching practices. For example, she forced her beginning students to spend hours a day copying the works of writers such as Hemingway, Faulkner and Fitzgerald. She forbade cross-fertilization of ideas, and kept the colonists — males, all — apart as much as she could. However, she took at least one of her students — Jones, 17 years her junior

— as a lover.

There is an essential difference between a room of your own — and everything else. Virginia Woolf articulated this famously. In a room of your own, you are an individual; everywhere else, you are colonized. The colonial mentality ruins the colonizers and the natives alike. Yes, the blandishments are amazing: tenure, if the colony is a university; a stipend and a month away from your day job, if the colony is in the woods of Maine or New Hampshire; plenty of sex and knowing winks if the colony is a circle, a clique, or a movement. But ruination is always lurking.

These perks are not to be sneezed at. Who wouldn't want the camaraderie (if that's what it is) and the free lunches (if there's any such thing) to be found in colonies? Who (besides me) wouldn't want that old fellow in uniform coming through sweeping and dusting? Who wouldn't want the blazing fire, the bottle of brandy, the modulated silence, the puns and the games, the readings and the chats? Who, when it comes down to it, wouldn't want to rule India? Well, not me, but I'm sure there are lots of takers.

If you are one of those takers, keep an eye on your writing. If it becomes anemic, fawning, arch, and sterile, you have been colonized. If you can't get a word out, if you have your PhD from a great university but can't write even an article, take note. You may be colonized and bamboozled. It won't look like the British in India, the Spanish in Mexico, or America everywhere. Rather, it will look exactly like you   you perusing an arcane journal, one in which you are supposed to publish, and feeling nothing but ennui and acid in your stomach.

Better a simple cottage and a mad landlord. Better freedom. Better independence, that backbone kind of thing. It takes no special skill with words to tell some decent truths. You only have to be braver than your neighbors. You only have to say, "I am independent" and mean it. You only have to remember the colonial history of the world. You only have to stand up — that's the main thing.

How many writers are not writing because they fear coming off as indecorous, ungrateful, impolite, even traitorous? How many writers are not writing because they fear something they would never confess to if they were asked directly — their own independence? How many writers are stalled because somewhere inside them a little voice is saying, "You know, you don't really have permission to say that." I suspect that the number is very large, maybe in the millions, maybe as large a number as the number of people in flocks and congregations.

Until our species leaves this earth, there will always be colonial masters and independent writers. There will be far more of the former and an infinite number of their followers; but there will also be a handful of the latter. They will want friends, they will want lovers, they will want publishers, but above all they will want to remain independent observers and reliable witnesses. And they won't mind an occasional landlord like Pop Demarest!

Mick Sinclair explained in *San Francisco: A Cultural and Literary History*: "The enchantment of Macondray Lane is now a well-shared secret. This wooded section of Russian Hill, with its vines, century-old trees, and quaint cottages, was home to many legendary writers, including Bret Harte, Pop Demarest, and Mark Twain. In the compound of small cottages that still populate this neighborhood, it's no wonder that art would flourish." Since it is not clear that Pop Demarest ever wrote a sentence, it is more than hyperbole to call him a legendary writer. But it is also a fitting reward for the perfect landlord.

CHRISTMAS AT MICHAEL'S

THERE WAS A TIME SOME YEARS AGO when San Francisco literary agent Michael Larsen was my agent. He liked to represent nonfiction projects, while his life partner and fellow agent, Elizabeth Pomada, represented novels. Every Christmas Michael and Elizabeth would throw a party at their Victorian flat for their clients. It was at one of these parties that the following horrible thing occurred.

I was talking to a fellow writer. He had written a novel that Elizabeth was representing, a thriller set in the Silicon Valley. He remarked that Elizabeth would be sending the novel out just as soon as he got his fiction proposal together. He was working on that right now.

"Your fiction proposal?" I said. I knew that nonfiction books were sold on the basis of proposals, and I had sold twenty books that way myself. In the world of fiction, however, the manuscript was everything. The novel sold itself or it didn't; its life didn't hinge on the author's marketing plan, credentials, platform, or other sales and marketing niceties. Had all that changed while I wasn't looking? Was the fiction proposal something new? I asked him.

"Yes," he replied in a conspiratorial whisper. This was indeed a new idea — selling fiction just the way you sold nonfiction, by pledging the moon and throwing money at the public. "I'm going to say in the proposal that I will put my *entire* advance toward publicizing the novel. If they give me thirty thousand, say, I will spend that whole thirty thousand on advertising. Since other novelists don't know to propose such a thing, I am going to have *such* a leg up!"

Just like that, the enterprise of hawking novels to editors looked to have transformed itself. This accountant knew better than to bank on the goodness of his writing. He was moving novel-writing into the twenty-first century, making it thoroughly American. Now you could say to an acquiring editor, "My novel may not have a voice or any integrity, but I will promote it with *real dollars.* So take *me!*" How could an editor resist? Wasn't there pressure on her to sell, just as there was pressure on everybody else? How could she turn down a rabid promoter willing to throw his advance into advertising?

I must admit to a certain unfortunate bias. I see nonfiction as practical and fiction as sacred. Nonfiction is like a steam engine, pulling good words to market. Fiction is like an eagle soaring overhead. In truth, this is a myopic, muddled distinction, since beautiful nonfiction is more soulful than stupid fiction and, to make matters worse, I've written at length about the folly of making these sorts of distinctions. But I was born a novelist, and childhood romanticism dies hard. To think that fiction was to become like nonfiction, open to the highest bidder, made me a little crazy.

"Did I mention that I'm an accountant?" he said. "I'm going to put that in the proposal, too. I want an editor to understand that I'm easy with the business end of writing." He leaned forward. "I pity any novelist who thinks that he can make it on the merits of his novel!"

I remembered a move from karate, the one where you drive the palm of your hand through your adversary's nose, pushing his nose bone into his skull. How fortunate for this accountant that I had my hands full with wine and cheese. Nor would a jury of my peers have found me guilty — a jury of novelists, that is.

I needed to find Michael and beg him to stop the madness. But Michael was already drumming. At a certain point during his parties, Michael always began drumming. Not New Age drumming on a tom-tom, but jazz drumming on a full set. I wanted to tell him, "Do not go in the direction of the fiction proposal! Do not allow it! Do not go down that awful road!" But he had his eyes shut and was brushing the drums. I didn't feel up to breaking his trance.

The accountant was sanguine that his plan would work. Since other novelists hadn't caught on yet, he had this amazing head start. He saw a clear path to six figures and — I saw it register, the lightbulb go on — why not seven? Yes! There were an infinite number of marketing ideas that he could cram into his proposal. There were things to give away, people to approach, brochures to create. Money begot money. He would spend, spend, spend and make his fortune at writing.

I said to myself, "There must be a Sufi tale about this." Some whirling dervish novelist somewhere must have written a fable about an accountant and the devil supping at an oasis just east of Kazakhstan. The devil says to the accountant, "You know, novelists think that it's all about the words!" They crack up laughing. They clink glasses. The accountant, tears in his eyes, replies, "And they don't even know to audit their publisher!" They howl! They slap each other hard on the back; and then the dancing girls appear.

Nonfiction book proposals remain the custom of the trade. That is the way you sell nonfiction, and I can live with that. Fortunately, fiction proposals do not seem to have caught on yet. Editors appear to be holding out; or maybe they tried a few novels written by accountants and discovered that readers couldn't be bought, or at least not bought that easily. For now, it appears that words still matter. But one day soon, since it has a market-driven inevitability to it, you will begin to hear that you can't sell a novel without writing a fiction proposal first.

On that day, the bones of novelists moldering in a million unmarked graves will rattle. It was hard enough to begin with, to write a good novel and to interest an editor in it. To suddenly have to compete with accountants who are throwing their advances at publicists is really the last straw.

19.

NOTHING THERE, A PARABLE OR RIDDLE

YOU WALK INTO YOUR KITCHEN. The coffeepot is there, the sink is there, the refrigerator is there. How comforting. You walk into your study, boot up the computer, stare at the blank screen. Nothing there. You leave your study. Another day of not writing.

You go to the bar. Lots of people there. Somebody orders champagne. Bodies dance in tight spaces. Very comforting. Between sips of champagne you wonder if you have a novel to write. No, nothing there. Another day of not writing.

Your arm is hurting. Maybe it's tendonitis. Maybe it's bursitis. Hard to say. But the pain is there, sharp as a nail. Something's there. You go into your study, boot up the computer, but your arm is hurting. Nothing there. Another day of not writing.

Where is your novel? Where is it hiding?

Somebody says, "An angel will bring it." You nod at that, because it reminds you of Christmas. Surely that's where your novel is, coming with an angel. But your angel must be busy bringing novels to other people. You can tell that she's not within a thousand miles of your townhouse. Nothing there, except more waiting.

Somebody says, "Your novel is at a workshop." You go to the workshop, called A Novel Workshop. As you sit there, doing exercises, something like your novel darts by, quick as a mouse, so quick that you aren't sure you really saw anything. Probably it was nothing. Back to the exercise, about your favorite adjectives. Nothing there.

Somebody says, "Probably you haven't got a novel in you. Probably you're sterile, like the rest of us." That makes sense to you. You feel sterile, so that must be it. You haven't got the egg, the sperm, the spark, the something. That's it, of course. Sterility. It reminds you of the look of your hometown. As sterile as that. Nothing was there, so nothing is in you, period.

A little boy says, "Tell me a story."

"About what?" you reply.

"I don't know. Make it up."

You make up a story. Something is there. But it is a story for children, lovely and tender but not your novel. Something is there, but is it more like something or more like nothing? Your stomach is churning. Something has been activated, but is it only stomach acid? You come up with a plan.

You go to a friend. You say, "Tell me to tell you a story."

"Excuse me?"

"Tell me to tell you a story."

"About what?"

"No, no! Just ask me to tell you a story."

"There's a story you want to tell me?"

"No, no! There's no story yet. But if you ask me to tell you a story, I think a story will come."

"I have to leave for the hairdresser's in thirty minutes. Will it be a long story?"

"I don't know! Just ask me to tell you a story!"

"Oh, for heaven's sake! Tell me a story."

Nothing there. Your friend is too impatient. She has only twenty-nine minutes left. Twenty-eight. You both look at the clock. Twenty-seven.

"You want me to tell you a story?" your friend finally says. "You know Adele, that really difficult woman at work? Just yesterday — "

"No!"

"Well, all right. So let's have your story."

You get up and leave abruptly.

You cry and have a bad month. It is a very bad month. You walk to the edge of a cliff overlooking the Pacific Ocean. The roar of the ocean drowns out the squawking of the gulls. There are whales out there, and seals, but who cares. You do not jump, but you come very close. The fog rolling in sends you shivering back to your car. You decide to stop looking.

A week later you change your mind. You ask the Zen master down the block, "Where is my novel?" He replies, "When you are empty, you are full." Could be. But he has never written a novel, and his dharma talks are incoherent. You try the master of Tao across the street. "Where is my novel?" you ask. "Every stage of the Way has its own Way," he replies. Could be. But he has never written a novel, and you wonder about the gold fixtures in his bathroom.

You try the cognitive therapist across town. "Where is my novel?" you ask. "Let's contract for a thousand words a day," she replies. "A thousand words of what?" you ask. "A thousand words of your novel," she replies. She is very cheerful. "But I don't have a novel!" you persist. "Then a thousand words of anything." "But I don't want a thousand words of anything." She smiles radiantly. "Would you like to pay me now, or shall I bill you?"

You take a jewelry-making class. "Maybe my novel is hiding in silver solder," you think. You make a silver elephant pendant that is resonant and beautiful. But your novel doesn't seem to be hiding there. That evening you rent a French movie. "French movies always move me," you say. "Maybe my novel is hiding there." You love the film, cry a little, and pledge to get back to Paris. But your novel wasn't hiding in the movie.

A year goes by. Day after day, nothing is there. You've been busy, idle, sober, drunk, happy, sad, everything, except writing. Finally you meet St. Peter at the Pearly Gates.

"Where was my novel hiding?" you ask plaintively.

"What novel?" St. Peter replies.

"The one I thought I was fated to write."

"The one you were fated to write!" St. Peter chuckles. "Didn't you get the part about free will? You were free to write a novel, not fated to write a novel."

"I still don't get it," you murmur, shaking your head. "Where was my novel?"

"Certainly not here," St. Peter replies testily, shutting the door behind you with a loud click.

20.

LYING AT THE TOP OF THE MARK

THE MARK HOPKINS IS A FANCY HOTEL at the crest of Nob Hill and the intersection of three cable car lines. At the hotel's summit is a celebrated bar where, during World War II, soldiers would drink before embarking and soldiers' wives would come to watch their husbands sail off toward Japan. Because of these wives, many of whom would soon become widows, the northwest corner of the room, with its views of the Golden Gate Bridge and the Pacific Ocean, became known as Weepers' Corner.

One afternoon in 1996, it should have been renamed Liar's Corner. I was meeting with Jeremy Tarcher, my publisher, and Irene Prokop, his editor in chief. They were in town for some reason, he from Los Angeles, she from New York, and found time to have drinks and dinner with me. None of us had an agenda — I wasn't trying to sell them a book, and they had no good or bad news to deliver. So it might have been a pleasant few hours, except for all the lies I was telling.

I had just signed on to do my fourth book with Tarcher, a book called *Lighting the Way*, an ambitious book about, well, everything. Don't look for *Lighting the Way* in bookstores. You won't find it. It was never published. The book's conceit, that it would do the best job ever of explicating human psychology and human meaning, wasn't the problem. The problem was in the execution. I couldn't get my hands around the material, so I busied myself taking illegitimate dodges and shortcuts. Then I lied to myself, along the following lines: "Hey, maybe nobody will notice!"

Irene, Jeremy, and I were chatting about one thing and another, and then Irene asked, innocently enough, since she had no suspicions, "How's the book going?"

"Great!" I replied. "Just great."

I have never told a bigger lie. I quickly changed the subject. They were none the wiser. We left the Top of the Mark and took a cab to a fancy Japanese restaurant, where we had an expense-account dinner. Some months later I turned in *Lighting the Way*. It was awful; naturally enough, they refused to publish it. It was not even in the kind of shape that would allow anyone at Tarcher to suggest a feasible rewrite. In another setting it would have been *Ishtar* or *Heaven's Gate*, only never released.

Of course writers will turn out clunkers. Some percentage of our books will stink. And sometimes we won't know that we have produced a stinker. What interests me is that defensive attitude, commonly called denial, that allows a writer who knows that his current book is flawed and who has no intention of owning up to that truth to continue writing, month in and month out, throwing bad words after bad. Why do we do that? It is such a waste of our essence, our spirit, our good ideas, our capital. Why do we do it?

Since I have done just that, with *Lighting the Way* and with some other books, let me see if I can explain what was going on for me. In each case part of me actually liked the book, or rather, liked the parts I liked. I was giving the book a pass because of its good parts. Part of me was unsure that anyone would notice, with so many bad books regularly being published. I was giving the book a pass because I felt smug and superior. Part of me hoped that, at some point, I would take the bull by the horns and do a real rewrite. I was giving the book a pass because I felt that I would yet rise to the occasion.

Part of me wondered if a miracle might happen, a gestalt miracle with the proper image suddenly emerging out of a murky background. Part of me was simply going through the motions, carried on by the momentum of getting up, writing the book, and going to bed, robot-like. Part of me didn't know what to do to make the book better and didn't want to admit that. Most tellingly, part of me just didn't care — one way or the other — and really didn't want to admit that.

To summarize: I lied to myself about how miserable *Lighting the Way* was turning out because I liked its good parts, felt smug and superior, imagined that I would yet rise to the occasion, was hoping for a miracle, was going through the motions, didn't know how to make it better, and didn't care, as in rhymes with despair. Do you ever do such things? Do you ever spend years on a book trying to ignore its smell? If you've never had this experience, you haven't written enough.

Do not leave a good book too soon or a bad book too late. The question naturally becomes: Which book is which? Maybe it's impossible to know. You are working on a book, you have your doubts, you have your hopes, and you just can't decide whether to go with hope or go with doubt. I understand. I find no easy solution wanting to come out of my pen. Maybe the closest I can come is the following: honorably rewrite. It is the *honorably* that makes the phrase so poignant.

I have never gone back to the Top of the Mark. For me it remains the scene of the crime. If you are currently lying about the book in front of you, the one you know is dead as a doornail and not worth two figs of your time, I understand. Denial is not just a river in Egypt. It is the way we keep up-to-the-minute news from pounding us like sledgehammer blows. In case you would like to tell yourself the truth and take your medicine, take a deep breath first. A lot of pain will follow, but also a better book, either this one or the next.

21.

THE FASTIDIOUS SURGEON

THE FASTIDIOUS, OVERBOOKED EYE SURGEON came down the hill from the University of California Medical Center on the heights of Parnassus to the Canvas Café on Ninth Avenue for our coaching session.

I'd gotten there early to walk in Golden Gate Park, directly across the street from the café, and to survey the art for sale on the café walls, art a full magnitude better than that found in most cafés. The Canvas Café has made a deserved name for itself as a real gallery. I carried my coffee cup around, enjoying the ladies' slips firmed up and turned into sculptures and the brilliant red abstractions. Finally I sat down and did a little writing.

My client arrived late, offered a perfunctory apology, and launched into his story. As an eye surgeon, he knew what he was doing. As a novice writer, working on his first novel, he had no idea what he was doing. Not knowing how to proceed with his novel, he hadn't. I noticed that he was very neat — trim, pressed, careful with his words, a napkin at the ready to take care of crumbs and spills — and made a mental note of the obvious problem. Neatness and novel-writing are mortal enemies. If Bob wanted to write his novel, he was first going to have to kill off the napkin-carrying part of his being.

I smiled and listened. I knew what he would say before he said it, but I allowed him to say it anyway. He told me some eye surgeon war stories that would have made a torturer squeamish, stories about roaming eyeballs and microincisions, and complained that he needed novel-writing to be more like eye surgery.

"But they are different things," I said.

"I know they're different things."

"No, you don't. You think they are the same thing, only different. But they aren't the same thing, only different. They're different things."

That caused him to pause. "Explain that," he said.

"Let's say that I set up my medical school to slightly differ from the ordinary medical school. In my medical school, I would send you, a protodoctor with no scalpel experience whatsoever, scores of patients and their eyeballs. I would say to you, 'Cut, have fun, see what you can learn. If you blind a few people, no problem. If you blind them all, no problem. The main thing is that you learn by doing, without a teacher, without any instruction at all. Enjoy!'"

"Medical school was exactly like that."

"Right."

He thought about what I was saying.

"Why the 'no teacher, no instruction' injunction? Why not take a workshop, study with someone, get some grounding?"

"Because of the basic difference. In surgery, you do not invite messes. You study so as to not make a mess. In novel-writing, you allow yourself to trip over your feet. Surgery is about not making a big mess, and writing is about tripping along and taking some pratfalls. Instruction helps you not make a big mess. It is therefore the wrong approach to novel-writing."

"You're being ironic."

"Am I?"

"You're being something."

"Let me get us a refill."

I noticed that he followed me up to the counter. I got us refills. He got us more napkins.

"Let me put it another way," I said when we were seated again. "There's a medical license. And then there's creative license. Do they sound like the same thing to you?"

Bob shook his head and laughed. "They really do not." He glanced at me. "So what am I supposed to do?"

"Something that you are not supposed to with the eyeballs of your patients. Something that you are clearly not comfortable doing anywhere. You have to forego neatness. If you want lines to come out pressed and sweet smelling, as if you had just picked them up from a fancy dry cleaner, you are killing your soul before you get started."

"Then there's this other thing," he murmured. "The novel has a lot of gay sex. Some masochism. Some sadism. Some bondage. Nothing that I'm embarrassed about, but it does get graphic..."

"And?"

"And — I don't know." He shook his head and smiled wanly. "I'm a respected eye surgeon."

"Yes. Who doesn't dare reveal the messy parts of his psyche and his reality?"

"Is that it?"

"Why else are you whispering?"

He shot a glance around.

"Say it out loud, if you like," I offered. "'I have sex, and sometimes it's really messy!' Or, 'My hands are clean when I cut your eyes but not in the middle of night, not by a damned sight!' Shout it out, if you like. It would help. And it certainly wouldn't disturb anybody here, not in a café in San Francisco!"

But he couldn't.

"So your mother will read your novel," I continued, "and your brother, and your co-workers, and they will think exactly what you fear they will think, that Bob is really messy inside, despite his clean-cut appearance. The process is messy, and what you are revealing is messy. Two messes for the price of one! That's my diagnosis."

"And the treatment?"

"Make those messes."

Bob sighed. "Well, thanks anyway. I've got to get back." He paused. "At least you haven't used Freudian jargon on me."

"You mean, I haven't called you anal?"

"Indeed."

"Your patients need you to wash your hands. There's no joking about that. But your novel needs you to get down and dirty."

Bob nodded. Then he was gone.

I took a last tour of the café paintings, left the Canvas, and crossed over to Golden Gate Park. On the field, a serious game of baseball was in progress, so serious that the players wore uniforms. The pitcher pitched, the batter swung, and the ball shot at the first baseman. A hard shot but an easy chance: still, the first baseman missed the ball. Error! What a word. *Error*. The very sound of it makes you not want to play the game.

22.

KIPLING AND DESIRE

RUDYARD KIPLING DID NOT FALL IN LOVE with San Francisco when he visited her in 1889. But he did fall in love with every woman he met here. A sly Rudyard explained, "I am hopelessly in love with about eight American maidens — all perfectly delightful till the next one comes into the room. The girls of America are above and beyond those of Europe. They are clever; they can talk; yea, it is said that they think. Certainly they have an appearance of so doing."

Whether he desired them for their brains or their bodies must remain Rudyard's little secret. What is clear is that he desired them. That makes perfect sense, since a prolific Rudyard and a horny Rudyard are two sides of the same coin. Out of desire comes lust, and out of desire comes a book. To better understand this connection let us start very far back, with the creation of the universe.

Front and center in our genetic memory is the experience of worlds arising out of nuclear explosions and flying gas. Some worlds, like Mercury, were made very hot; some, like Jupiter, were made very cold. Some, like our earth, gave rise to apple orchards, mosquitoes, and us. We have the knowledge of this odd occurrence as a deep genetic reality, maybe the deepest and most real, this long-ago-but-still-evolving creation of the coherent, sometimes beautiful globe on which we live.

Because of this genetic understanding, we feel a peculiar pressure to replicate creation. We see that, out of nothing much, just strings and process, a world with mountain chains, moonbeams, and Rotarians arises. Something itchy like desire gets us thinking that we should make a world, too. It feels like the very best use of our time on earth and a way to mimic other blessed creators. We say, "Gee, I can build some worlds. Bring it on!"

So we begin. The second step in creating this new world is to collect some matter, since even gods need matter in order to make their visions manifest. Our matter is comprised of ideas, images, feelings, words, and other conventional-sounding building blocks. But more fundamental than those is the desire that caused us to embark on the collecting.

Our desire to create a world is analogous to the energy that causes strings to vibrate and that permits matter to come together. The instant our desire stops, our world-building ends. The instant our desire returns, we find ourselves at play again in the fields of words. Even gods must reckon with this fundamental relationship between a mass (like a book) and energy (like desire). Could a bored god create a solar system? Can you cause Boise in the 1890s to materialize without a real desire to do so?

Focus on desire, then! If you do, you will be able to think much more clearly about the stages of a book. The first stage, which is world-building (often misnamed incubation), is that genetic-based desire to build a world translated into a first pushing and pulling of mind matter. It is all taffy and electrons; we start the taffy-pull. We say, "Go, brain!" The machine turns on, and at some point, having stretched the taffy and collected electrons into meaning, it produces something recognizable, like "Havana, 1945." The world we intend to build is suddenly known to us.

Our shorthand term for this process is "thinking." But it is better conceptualized as world-building and taffy-pulling fueled by high-voltage desire. It is a real process, like taffy-pulling, arising out of a real goal, to make a world, fueled by real energy, the energy of desire. If you haven't the goal, then nada. If you avoid the process, then nada. If you are low on desire or, worse, bereft of desire, then nada. The equation: desire, aimed at a goal, produces a world.

Suddenly you have a mass of matter and must work it. As likely as not, the pieces do not easily go together, and your god skills are tested. You have plaster in the batter, the mosquitoes you invented fly but will not bite, the taffy that you expected would turn out pink is a sickly yellow. None of that is a problem to a world-builder like you — except that, because of the difficulties, your desire wanes. Your strings stop vibrating. You get mundanely human and slip from world-builder to newspaper-reader. Your book becomes like Jupiter, inert and cold.

The complete solution? That you rekindle your desire. For every stage of the book-writing process, the complete solution to the problems that arise is the rekindling of goal-oriented desire. If the problem is that a character is flat, you rekindle your desire to breathe life into her. If the problem is that it is time to write a synopsis of your novel and the absurdity of that task demoralizes you, you rekindle your desire to present your world to the public. If the problem is that chapter 3 is excellent but chapter 4 is stupid, you rekindle your desire to make your world work, just as a committed god does when she notices that her short-necked giraffes can't reach the upper leaves. You make chapter 4 better. A god doesn't leave her giraffe in the lurch. Will you?

There are reasons why writers who write a lot, as Rudyard did, have big appetites. They are dancing bundles of desire. Writers who write crave sex, peanuts, and Nobel Prizes. They crave; they itch; they lust; they are alive. Whether they manage this mélange of desires well is a separate matter. But without this dancing, pressing desire they would sit quietly like old folks lined up in the corridor of a nursing home. Honor your goal to create a world by burning with desire. Be incandescent — or nothing will happen.

Here is our little creation ditty, then, something like a simplified version of the Babylonian Genesis:

I am a world-builder.
That isn't so easy.
But I am a world-builder.
Even with all my disabilities.
I am a world-builder.
Desire is the complete prescription.
Whether I find myself on stage one of my book, stage two, or stage
    one hundred.
Without desire I am done.
So every day I rekindle my desire. Somehow.

Rudyard Kipling had little trouble rekindling his desire daily. "I cannot write connectedly," Rudyard lamented as his San Francisco visit neared its end, "because I am in love with all those girls aforesaid and some others who do not appear on the invoice." Ah, Rudyard, have your little joke. We know that, flooded with desire, you could write connectedly just fine.

PARENTING SKILLS
FOR STAY-AT-HOME WRITERS

IF I ASKED YOU HOW you'd ideally like to spend an hour, you would probably reply, by quietly writing. If an observer watched you as you sat there quietly writing, he might see you eating a grape, staring into space, doodling on the pad beside your computer, and every so often clacking away with lightning speed at your computer keyboard. He would not see you typing for sixty minutes straight. Most of the time you would just be sitting there, which is exactly as it should be.

You would just be sitting there, canalizing your energy, focusing your being, and sometimes typing. What bliss! What perfection! Every writer knows that state of staring into space and occasionally transcribing. When a writer then turns to parenting her children, however, an entirely different model steals her brain. Her personal heaven is sitting quietly; her child, she mistakenly thinks, must be kept busy. Her child must do his homework, his piano lessons, his French translations, his chores, and everything else that will make him successful and accomplished. If he is caught staring into space, she is inclined to cry, "Don't you have homework?"

A kind of cultural anxiety overcomes this otherwise soulful writer. She is anxious that her child be this thing called "successful," even though she herself would never measure her life in such terms. Something in her psyche that is not her own voice tells her that her child must seize his opportunities, climb the ladder, and ace his math test. She feels an intense pressure to push him and something like an obligation to get him on the fast track. "Faster, Johnny! Faster! Mary is twenty yards closer than you to Harvard!"

I would like to present another model, one much closer to the writer's actual heart. Whipping children into a frenzy of activity and demanding that they earn their seat at the table by their accomplishments are not the only ways to create ambitious children. Nor are they the healthiest. If you have the luxury of being a stay-at-home writer and parent, you have the opportunity to try a radically different approach. You can treat your kids as you would like to be treated.

What did you want as a child? A quiet environment. Freedom from chaos and conflict. A window seat, a view, and a pad and pencil. Some music. The chance to make mistakes without anyone caring. The chance to fry ants with your magnifying glass, chew on some blades of grass, and stick beans in your ears. Books to read. A Saturday movie. French fries.

Nothing mysterious, nothing theoretical. Can't you extrapolate from this vision of your ideal childhood exactly how to parent?

You write for an hour while your child makes a mess with Play-Doh. You write for an hour while your child reads a book. You sit with your child and exchange stories. You write your book, and he writes his. No getting in the car; no driving anywhere; no forced marches to the piano teacher. All that driving steals precious hours from your writing time and does far less for your child than if he got to watch you quietly write. Better you model writing than send him to writing camp! Quietly write in the presence of your child, and foster genius.

I was the stay-at-home parent to our daughters, Natalya and Kira. Every day I would take them out in their double-stroller to San Francisco State, across the street from our apartment, and we would use that commuter university as our personal playground. We would roll on the grass. We would buy candy in the lobby shop of the student union. We would take the elevator up to the fifth floor of the library where, unbeknownst to the students on campus, a children's library lived. We would take out books and read them at home. Our favorite was the story of a French lamb named Patapon; our second favorite, *Lyle the Crocodile.*

On our way out the door to State, I would slip Kira's bottle into the back pocket of my jeans (a bottle will fit — try it). One day an irate African student stopped me and cried, "Sir, that is not sanitary!" I smiled. I would not baptize my children in the Ganges, since I know something about typhoid and dysentery, but I also know that a bottle in your back pocket is exactly as God intended it, just as long as you keep its cap on. It was no more unsanitary than carrying it in a designer pouch. I suspect that it was more the image of casual parenting — what may even have seemed to him like a mockery of parenting — that offended him.

During the day I would sing the girls songs (some of which, it turned out, scared them), cook pasta (many, many times a week), inexpertly do laundry, and inadvertently vacuum. Sometimes we would go to the playground tucked uphill behind the public library. Sometimes we went all the way to the zoo, where it was always foggy and atmospheric. Occasionally we hopped the streetcar for an in-town outing. And every day I would write.

Writing is a writer's prime parenting skill. If you don't write, you get sad, angry, unhinged, anxious, gloomy, pessimistic, and morose. By writing first thing in the morning, as your children play or toddle off to school, you put yourself in the mood to smile at them when next you see them. Writing is a tonic, an elixir, even if it goes badly, because even if it goes badly at least you have been writing.

I am pleased to say that this quiet, measured, writing-filled way did not ruin our daughters. To describe how well they are doing would be to brag and might also hex them, so I'll keep mum on that score. But they are able to laugh; they are able to love; and they are happiest writing. What else could a writer-parent want?

MARK TWAIN AND *THE ONION*

MARK TWAIN, A REPORTER for the *San Francisco Daily Morning Call* during the summer of 1864 and famously associated with San Francisco because of his remark about the coldness of that summer, did something in *Huckleberry Finn* that none of us have been able to do since. He made false advertising cost you your life.

Today, as always, hucksters are free to claim that you can lose your fat by applying a certain cream or that by killing some thousands over there you will improve your national security here. They are free to call a boy a hero because he was ordered into a building and shot dead and free to call his mother a scoundrel for doubting that her son was used well. You can't stop the hucksters; you never could, and you never will. But, as a writer, at least you can excoriate them.

The everyday conning that is today an art form so annoyed Twain that, in *Huckleberry Finn*, he created two memorable characters, the king and the duke, the very model of American con men — created them to get even just a little. Unlike our con men today, who, because they are ubiquitous, are invisible, and because they are entrenched, are invulnerable, the king and the duke get one royal comeuppance. Twain had them tarred and feathered and ridden out of town on a rail. Yes!

You may not be aware that Twain was exacting capital punishment. The tarring and feathering was one thing, and highly unpleasant. But the riding out of town on a rail was a whole lot worse. It wasn't that the outraged townsfolk whom the king and the duke scammed put them on the train and waved good-bye to them — they weren't put on *that* kind of rail. No, a stake was jammed up their respective backsides, and they were pogo-ed out of town. That harrowing ride was meant to kill them.

The palpable anger that rises up in a satirist like Twain, who is made insane by the shameless venality of the dupers and the identical shameless venality of the duper's victims — who crave having the wool pulled over their eyes so they can feel righteous about their own wool-pulling — is evidenced by his choice of such an unholy punishment. Would Twain the man ever have sentenced even a politician to rail-riding? Probably not. But Twain the writer could hardly wait. Boiling over, he was desperate to commit satire.

Fortunately for all of us, it has become something of a San Francisco tradition to satirize con men. It is probably one of our finest traditions, finer than ordering Ramos Gin Fizzes at brunch or trekking to

Chrissy Field for Fourth of July fireworks. When I walk down Mission Street I am bound to encounter, at a newsstand, *The Onion*. Yes! A satirical weekly born in Madison, Wisconsin, incubated on the Web, and available in a handful of cities, *The Onion* is pure Twain. It is Swift, Aristophanes, *Mother Jones*, *Mad* magazine, Beat rags, and leftie broadsides all rolled into one. You will get what *The Onion* is about from its headlines. To wit:

"Evangelical Scientists Refute Gravity with New 'Intelligent Falling' Theory."

"Calcutta Fire Marshal: Many Indian Homes Lack Bride Extinguisher."

"New Pepsi Negative-220 Burns Twice the Calories It Contains."

Naturally *The Onion* gets embroiled in every manner of lunacy. When it published a piece under the headline "Homosexual Recruitment Drive Nearing Goal," fundamentalists used the story as proof that gays were out to convert straights. To show evidence of the venality of Washington's finest, *The Beijing Evening News* reprinted portions of a story *The Onion* ran on Congress's threat to leave Washington for Memphis unless it got a new building with a retractable dome. Recently, newscasters have made fine use of *The Onion*'s statistic that "58 percent of all exercise done in the United States is done on television."

Twain would have loved this. But even his love of *The Onion* would not have helped relieve him of the bitterness that dogged his later years. Having lost his money on various printing and publishing debacles, forced to tour and lecture endlessly and be funny when he didn't feel funny, suffering the death of two of his daughters and the long illness and death of his wife, his geniality evaporated. His misanthropy, tempered in books like *Huckleberry Finn* by wry good humor, finally prevailed.

There is always the chance that a satirist's misanthropy will triumph. We are just human, after all, and can get worn down by all the patriots and salesmen, the scoundrels and church ladies, the advertisers and politicians. To repeatedly point out that the emperor has no clothes means that you must spend your life looking at naked emperors. That is demoralizing, disturbing, surreal, and tiring.

Some of our greatest satirists, among them Twain, Ambrose Bierce, Tom Wolfe, and H. L. Mencken, have made hay in San Francisco. Still, it gets tiring poking fun at clay-footed icons of the left and right, there being so many of them. The charming lilt of your sentences, as you make modest proposals and point out larcenies, is really not enough to keep you going. You need results; but you can't have results, human nature being what it is.

For thousands of years satirists have tried their damnedest to expose and shame the world's villains. Since they have had such limited success, you wouldn't want your child to become a satirist. Except, of course, that you would, since without a little satire the con men could claim a complete victory. Read your Twain; subscribe to *The Onion*; ready your darts.

RODIN AT THE LEGION OF HONOR

WHAT PIECE OF GENETIC CODE causes a husband to say to his wife, "I expect dinner on the table when I get home!"? Is it the same strand that makes a sister say to her brother, "I know that I'm going off to college, and I know that my room is nicer than your room, but you can't have my room when I leave!"? When Richard Dawkins wrote *The Selfish Gene*, it must have been this everyday selfishness that he had in mind. No person would do these things! — it must be our genes talking.

It is this selfsame shameless selfishness, rooted so deep that only the longest-handled scalpel can reach it, that prevents lovers from actually loving. Come with me, and I'll explain what I mean. Let's walk out to the Legion of Honor, a San Francisco museum on the ocean side of the city, high atop a golf course and overlooking the sea. We'll park near Nineteenth Avenue and walk along one of the Richmond streets, maybe along Geary Boulevard, where Russian and Chinese are spoken, or along Lake Street. Out Lake Street we will be compelled to stop at a certain deli, dropped, herring and all, from Minsk, where suspicious babushkas will cut us up some fresh-baked mushroom-and-onion strudel.

The walking is gray, this being the foggy end of San Francisco. But as we trudge uphill past the golf course we are likely to find the Legion of Honor bathed in sunlight, since it sits high up, higher up even than the houses along the cliffs of Sea Cliff, where Robin Williams may be heard laughing. It is sunny up here, serene, and a much more interesting place to jump than the Golden Gate Bridge. It is certainly a good spot to build a replica of Paris's Palais de la Legion d'Honneur, should you want to do that, which apparently Alma de Bretteville Spreckels, wife of San Francisco sugar magnate Adolph Spreckels, in fact did.

The Legion of Honor has a lovely café in which to write, a fine collection of monochromatic paintings for those of us who get a thrill from all-black canvases, a charming small concert hall for rarefied music, and a Rodin sculpture court right in the center. When I enter that center court, however, I never see the sculptures. I only see Rodin's transgressions. His failure to help his apprentice and lover, Camille Claudel, parlay her brilliance into fame obsesses me. It is a manifestation of that genetic selfishness that dooms all but the most evolved relationships.

The other day a client told me about her husband, who for the last few decades hasn't cared to work. She works for the both of them and also tries to write, but, surprise, surprise, doesn't get much writing done. Restless from so much not-working, her husband likes to hike and recently importuned my client to take a vacation in the mountains. She thought that she might get in some daydreaming and some writing, and so she agreed to the vacation. But when they got there he demanded that she hike. You would think that two twenty-first-century human beings could negotiate a way to make a beautiful day in the country beautiful for the both of them. But no. It had to be heavy backpacks straight up the hill, and damn the reverie.

Or consider that legendary moment some twenty years ago when a best-selling female author entered the monthly luncheon of some dozen venerable San Francisco male authors, looked around the room, and exclaimed, "I've sold more books than all of you put together!" Certainly it wasn't she who spoke! No doubt she was too kind and humane to say such a thing. It must have been her ventriloquist, those selfish genes, inoculating her to the gathered authors' disdain by getting the first blow in. As it so often happens when writers gather, this luncheon was no jolly lovefest.

Who are the villains? Not the people involved! — people would never do such things. A bad, old ancient gene in Rodin must have said, "Anyone else's success diminishes you, Auguste. Be very careful!" Rodin certainly must have known better — look at his *Kiss*, look at his *Thinker*. Surely he possessed evolved-enough feelings that generosity and compassion must have counted among them. But his damned rotten genes, like the snake in the Garden of Eden, kept hissing and whispering. That Camille went insane was no skin off his back!

My own selfish genes, too numerous to count, have been subdued or at least kept in line by my heartfelt appreciation of, first, my mother's support, and then my wife's. Blessed by that support, I became kinder than I otherwise would have been. Esther said, "Go ahead, write." Ann said, "Go ahead, write." So I have written for thirty-five years. Sitting at the café at the Legion of Honor, having a nice salad, thankful not to be oiling the machinery of reality in an office, I chide Rodin and must repeat, "Couldn't you have shared the spotlight with Camille?" You, Auguste, who had so much, ought to have known better.

Walking back from the Legion is easier than walking to it, since we are now heading downhill. We only have to remember where we parked the car, which was somewhere near the bagel place on Geary, wasn't it? Even in the fog, the gold onion-dome spires of the Russian Orthodox Church on Twenty-seventh Avenue gleam. I have no palate for the tea flavors of ice cream at the Japanese ice cream parlor at Eighteenth Avenue, but I do duck in for a donut at Donut World. Donut World is filled with old Chinese men drinking coffee. Another excellent place to write, the Styrofoam and Formica notwithstanding. It is not the Palais de la Legion d'Honneur or the Legion of Honor, but I feel altogether blessed.

REGARDING BLACKBIRDS

IT WAS 1981. Ann was pregnant with Natalya. I wrote a good novel that year, *The Blackbirds of Mulhouse*. I can picture us vacationing for a few days that summer at Lake Tahoe, at Camp Richardson, an inexpensive place with cold, bare cabins. I revised *Blackbirds* there and was happy with it. I remember reading the last page of the novel and feeling that tingle you get when a piece of writing has turned out well.

Then, in a laughably inept and insufficient way, I tried to interest agents and editors in it. It is possible that I approached as few as one or two agents and one or two editors. Not only did I approach too few marketplace players before giving up, I'm sure that I wrote an ironic, uninformative query letter bound to elicit zero interest. And I got no interest. It is fair to say that the novel was much better than my efforts at marketing it.

I had this good novel and, as I framed the matter to myself, no takers. So I decided to self-publish it. I saw myself in the tradition of Fyodor Dostoyevsky, James Joyce, Virginia Woolf, Stephen Crane, Mark Twain, William E. B. Dubois, D. H. Lawrence, and Henry David Thoreau, among many others. It probably struck me as a badge of honor to join writers like these who had stood up for their fiction by self-publishing. I saw what I was doing as heroic. I became a publisher, the Maya Press, spent a few thousand dollars, and made a book.

The cartons arrived at our apartment. I think the print run was two thousand, which fills a lot of cartons. (I have two-thirds of one carton left.) I put together a press release, tucked a copy of the release and a copy of *Blackbirds* in each of the two hundred manila envelopes, and sent them out to reviewers whose names and addresses appeared in *Literary Marketplace*. I had no other plan and no other ideas. I sat back and waited — maybe I even sat on one of those cartons, since they must have been everywhere in the apartment.

Those of you who are savvy about the marketing and reviewing of books will know that the following verges on the impossible. *Blackbirds* got many reviews. Giant publishing houses with their publicity apparatus and in-bed connections could not have done much better. The full-page *San Francisco Chronicle* review of *Blackbirds* ended as follows: "It is a pleasure to read a novel written so carefully, one in which the author has complete control of every detail and gesture, each turn of the plot. This is an engrossing, eloquent book." *Publisher's Weekly*, on its contents page, called it "an intriguing, sensitive psychological study." *The Midwest Book Review* concluded with the following uplifting sentence: "Tensions are introduced and built upon until the final tragic yet surprising conclusion, making *The Blackbirds of Mulhouse* a psychological drama not easily forgotten."

I offer up these quotes to brag, of course, but also to make sure that you understand that some things that are self-published are excellent. That isn't to say that a writer ought to leap to self-publishing. It is to say, however, that our everyday disdain for things like self-published novels, which we cavalierly imagine to be crap and their authors ridiculous failures, ought to stop. Dostoyevsky, Twain, Woolf, and Joyce are not inferior to novelists who get published. Agents and editors like to say that a good novel will always find a home, implying that every self-published or unpublished novel is bad. But they are just covering their backs and fibbing.

An interesting moment came a few years later. Ann, teaching English at Lick-Wilmerding High School, had just given birth to Kira. I went in for the semester to teach Ann's classes. One of the classes I got to teach was "The Modern Novel." I picked the reading list, opting for George Orwell, Virginia Woolf, André Malraux, Albert Camus, and other stalwarts — and included *Blackbirds*. I knew that it was a good novel, and I had no qualms. I felt sure that it would stand up to the "real" novels I was teaching.

In fact, it was a pure joy to teach *Blackbirds*. I would pose my students an essay question like, "What do you imagine the author intended by the scene where Martin finds himself unequal to buying cold cuts?" How can you not smile when you are "the author" and get to ask questions like that? Even better was reading their answers. Those essays confirmed that the ideas in *Blackbirds* were actually there on the page, clear and available.

One moment stands out. A student in my class was sitting on the floor in front of her locker, engrossed in reading *Blackbirds*. As I walked by, she looked up. You could read in her expression that she was not afraid to have an opinion. She nodded and said, "This is a lot better than I expected it would be." Out of the mouths of babes! Of course, you would not expect your high school substitute teacher's novel to match up to *Man's Fate* and *The Fall*. She hadn't; and it had.

As I write this, my fiction agent, Peter Riva, the grandson of Marlene Dietrich, is in Frankfurt at the annual international book fair, doing many things, among them trying to interest European publishers in *Blackbirds*. We shall see. I know it is a good novel, and I do not need other people to validate my opinion. On the other hand, I wouldn't mind having some readers. It will be interesting if it ends up taking thirty years for this novel to move from inception to reception. Having kept busy all these years, I haven't minded the wait that much.

27.

A SINGLE KOAN

SAN FRANCISCO IS THE ONLY EASTERN CITY IN AMERICA. Its bone- and blood-level connection to Japan, China, and a way of thinking alien to the rest of America is part of its attraction for writers. In honor of that connection, I offer the following.

The Zen Master Hakuin, a founding father of the Rinzai Sect of Zen Buddhism, famously said, "What is the true meditation? It is to make everything...into a single koan." During 2005 and 2006 I had seven nonfiction books published. People ask me, "Where do you get the energy?" But I have no special energy. I have just made everything into a single koan. If you want to write ten books, twenty books, thirty books, make everything into a single koan.

A koan is a riddle, a puzzle, an enigmatic response, a paradoxical statement or story used by Zen masters to confuse and confound their disciples and, presumably, to awaken them. The phrase "make everything into a single koan" is itself a koan. It hardly makes even metaphoric sense. It is designed to make you throw up your hands and shout, "Enough! I'll do it my way!" It is designed to free you.

Or perhaps a koan is the way that a Zen master binds you to him.

A young man asked the dharma teacher, "Since the Buddha said that Buddhism has nothing to teach, how can you be a teacher of Buddhism?"

"I teach that there is nothing to teach," the dharma teacher replied.

"But you teach that we need to practice."

"Practice is necessary."

"So you do teach something."

Unruffled, the dharma teacher said nothing.

"And you teach about detachment, compassionate action, and many other things," said the young man. "These may all be good things, but to say that you aren't teaching is a bald-faced lie. You teach all the time."

Again the dharma teacher made no reply.

"A Buddhist who teaches is a liar, even when what he teaches is the truth," the young man muttered to himself, vowing never to set foot in such a place again. Thus he stepped into his freedom.

An old woman sat outside her hovel, writing a poem. The church bells were ringing. People from the town strode past. "We are on our way to church," they announced. "Come join us!" When they saw her make no move to join them, they gathered around her and began crying, "Come along, come along, it's Sunday!"

The old woman shook her head. "I'm writing a poem for my granddaughter," she said.

"You can work on your poem later!" someone shouted.

"The sermon today is on compassion!" a second chimed in. "That can't be missed!"

"Do you want to anger the Holy Spirit?" cried a third. "And bring His wrath down on our village?"

The old woman shook her head. "Spirit is right here beside me," she said.

The townspeople cursed her and, when they came upon her writing a new poem the following Sunday, stoned her to death. At her funeral, some very beautiful poetry was read.

☖

A man thought to be very wise kept to himself. It was widely believed that he was more than a hundred years old, and it amazed people that he still tended to his own needs, walking without a cane to do his shopping and even stopping at the library to read, albeit with a magnifying glass.

One day some townspeople gathered around him.

"Do you believe in everlasting life?" they asked.

"No."

"Do you believe in heaven?"

"No."

"Do you believe that God will greet you when you die?"

"No."

"Then why are you smiling?"

"Because I suddenly thought of something that amuses me."

"What's that?" they cried, anticipating a pearl of wisdom.

"You've come to find out what I know, but you wouldn't listen to me if your life depended on it. Isn't that amusing?"

"But we *would* listen!" they cried. "We would!"

"Then this is what I have to teach you. The universe doesn't care about you. The only reason that you possess to do the right thing is that it is the right thing to do."

They left disappointed, muttering to themselves that God would surely get even with this old man — and pretty damned soon now.

॰

It would fly in the face of what I have just written to point you in the direction of the San Francisco Zen Center, one of the largest *sanghas* outside Asia, located at Page and Laguna Streets in Hayes Valley, or to mention their branches in the country, Green Gulch Farm in Marin and the Tassajara Zen Mountain Center inland from Big Sur. Just as you must kill the Buddha, you must burn down all Zen centers, even (or especially) one founded by Shunryu Suzuki Roshi, the Japanese priest who wrote *Zen Mind, Beginner's Mind*.

I hope you understand what I mean. If you think that I am suggesting murder and arson, then you don't. I mean the following. Someone must stand outside while everyone else is inside. The writer is likely that someone. Someone must say, "Every organization is self-serving." The writer is likely that someone. Someone must paint a picture not commissioned by a patron. The writer is likely that someone. Someone must indict all known religions and all religions to come, theistic or atheistic, as betrayals of our common humanity. The writer is likely that someone.

So I will not point you to any places of Eastern worship in San Francisco. If you are inclined to find them, you surely will. But before you go looking for a Shinto shrine, a Taoist hangout, a Confucian café, or a Buddhist temple, ask yourself the following three questions.

1. "Isn't temple-going always idolatry?"
2. "Isn't writing every day the best sitting meditation?"
3. "How can I live my life like a single koan if I am always giving my life away?"

COHEN FOR A DAY

WOMEN DO IT ALL THE TIME, when they marry. But most men never change their name. They are born John Jones and remain John Jones forever. To have a lasting identity wrapped around an enduring name is a comforting thing, no doubt, as good as old slippers, and maybe a psychological plus. But should a writer really grow that comfortable? Wouldn't it be nice to get out from under "Norman Mailer" or "John Updike" for a year or two? Wouldn't it be refreshing to suddenly become Norman O'Malley or John Goldfarb?

My name is Eric Maisel. That's pretty funny. In Bavaria, where there were Lutheran Maisels, the Jews were ordered to grab a German name. Some glommed onto Maisel. So Maisel, for a Jew like me, is already a so-to-speak slave name.

Then one Samuel Maisel made his way to America and married my mother, Esther Shapiro. That, of course, explains my name — if only Samuel Maisel hadn't died five years before I was born. The plot thickens.

Samuel Maisel died, leaving Esther with two small children, Marcia and Bob. Then Esther met the love of her life, David Cohane. This is another joke of naming, because David Cohane was born David Cohen but changed his name to Cohane to better his chances in New York City politics. I guess the idea was to pick a name so close to Cohen that you would get the Jewish vote but Irish enough that you would also get the Irish one.

Some fifteen years before meeting Esther, David pulled off what is really a staggering feat for a first-generation immigrant. He wrote a book and got it published. I possess what is probably the only extant copy of my father's book. It is called *Practical Political Procedure: A Guide for Party Workers* and was published in 1932 by the Meador Press of Boston. The Meador Press published books like *From Captivity to Fame: The Life of George Washington Carver* and *John Jacob Astor: An Unwritten Chapter.* And my father's book.

It has a beautiful frontispiece photo of him — he was a handsome fellow, a cavalryman in World War I, someone who liked to bet on horses. The book begins with this dedication: "To the vast army of political workers, especially the local election district Committeemen and women." Next follows what my father called "My Patriotic Pledge." It is made up of fifteen items; here are six of them:

I will love my country which has redeemed me from tyranny
and bondage.

I will always strive to be patriotic, and not use patriotism to
hide any selfish motive.

I shall exercise the duties of a free man in order to safeguard the
principles of freedom.

I will never seek a public office which I am not fit to fill.

I will never be indifferent to the acts of unworthy public office
holders.

I shall dedicate myself to the service of human life, human
liberty, and human happiness.

I met my father once, for a handful of minutes. I was thirteen and
already shaving. Either my mother didn't know that I was shaving
and thought I could use some lessons, or else she knew and was afraid
that I'd slit my throat without some mentoring. One day a man appeared, the only man ever to turn up in our apartment. I was in the
bathroom, shaving. The man came to the bathroom door and wondered if I needed any instruction. I replied, "No, I know what I'm
doing." I'm not sure we exchanged another word.

Years later — maybe decades later — I learned that the man who'd
appeared at the bathroom door that day was my father. I had no real rec-
ollection of him and no need for one. Years after that my sister told me
some stories — that David was a kind man, that he had been nice to Bob
and her, that he always brought her a present when he visited, that he
was very handsome and masculine. As Marcia told the story, David and
Esther were very much in love but he gambled, lost her money, and she
threw him out. I was only months old, or not even born yet.

The first time my mother mentioned my father was when I was
about twenty-three or twenty-four. I was working on my first novel and

announced that fact. Esther's reaction was a cross between wry and fatalistic.

"You know, your father was a writer," she said.

Having never in my life heard a word about my father, this was as rhetorical as a comment could get. I waited.

"Something about politics," she continued. "I have his book." She looked at me. "You should keep it. It must be in the genes."

In one fell swoop I had a father, a genetic legacy, and a literary tradition. I don't know what I felt in the moment, but I'm sure that it wasn't anything simple like joy, pride, or consternation. It still isn't anything simple. It's like a name: Eric Maisel. How simple is that?

29

TEN THOUSAND DAYS AND COUNTING

I'M WRITING THIS PIECE at Progressive Grounds in Bernal Heights. In a few minutes I'll meet with a client, a writer who can't find the wherewithal to start on her third novel because her first two novels have gone out of print. Her heart is hurting. Well, we will chat, and I will try to help her heal. If immediate healing isn't possible, at least we will be out of the fog, in a warm café, talking about something important, namely, her writing.

I am having a "small" cup of coffee, which is actually an enormous one, filling a café au lait mug. I am also having a pumpkin confection with white icing, which I shouldn't be. I am doing what I have done virtually every day for ten thousand days, sitting and writing. It is nothing special to look at, though, as Gunther Grass once remarked, books are stronger than frontiers. You could write something and bring down the Great Wall of China. But to an observer you would look just like this — a person sitting, nodding, staring, and scribbling.

In those ten thousand days of writing I wish I had accomplished much more. Many good books eluded me. Many good books I failed. For some, I needed thirty more IQ points than I possess. For others, I needed more patience or better resolve. Some went well. Some were excellent. Still, I would have liked to have done much more. I doubt that we are so very different in that regard, you and me. You know the vast quantity and quality of books you had within you. I bet you would have liked to have done more, too.

I talked to another client today on the phone. She is a painter, and her work is beautiful. But she isn't painting because her alcoholic son is being crazy and has dragged her into it. She can't say no, even though her own health is at risk. In the middle of this madness, what is on her mind is what is always on our minds: I have good work to do, and I wish I were doing it. She doesn't begrudge her son anything. It is only that his turmoil is a theft, stealing the peace of mind necessary to levitate paintings.

She needs to be painting because she has a soul. Do not take that to be a statement about gods or spirits — for it is a statement about humanity. A botched novel produces a river of tears because the human soul, wanting that novel, is beside itself with grief. It isn't ego that needed that novel to soar. All ego needed was for that novel to sell. No, it was soul, human soul, some odd spandrel, some artifact of evolution, some breathing of the universe coursing through this perverse life-form, you and me. We cry for our ruined novels, and we cry for our fine books; that's how soul operates.

If a ruined novel brings on tears, what does not writing produce? A personal ice age. How many writers, not having written, have rushed out to a warm bar to thaw out a little? Here in San Francisco that writer might have taken the chill off with a Hot Toddy at the Orbit Room or with an Irish Coffee at the Buena Vista. He might have done the trick with a Bohemian Coffee at Vesuvio's or with a Nutty Irishmen at the Edinburgh Castle. Very nice! — but hardly the right medicine.

The soul, chronically ill because it must reckon with death, with the reality of evil, with every manner of pain and indignity, can never be cured of what ails it. It can be soothed a little, though. It isn't the Bohemian Coffee or the Hot Toddy that will soothe it. It is the righteous work, always falling short, that the artist attempts. You write a little, soothe your soul, and maybe cry bitterly, the way you do when you listen to Chopin.

I saw two clients last week, a young man and a young woman, each of whom had a thousand ideas. Each wanted to combine images, words, feelings, fashion, art, life, everything. Each wanted to make something like a tapestry, only not a tapestry, or something like a book, only not a book, or something like pure process, whatever that might mean, or something like a gallery show or an event or a performance or... I knew what they were saying. They were saying, "I have a soul, and it is bursting." I had to tell them both, "You must choose."

The soul demands immortality and a feast, and all a mortal can do is bring it a peach. But better bring it that peach! — or else you will disappoint it even more. Write the book, even though it is only a book. Write the next book, even though it is only another book. Do the thing that is more beneficial than prayer, more honest than praise, more humble than apologetics, more noble than martyrdom. Do the writing your soul requires. It isn't enough; but less is worse.

There is still tomorrow and always tomorrow. Maybe I'll spend a few hours at Muddy's on Valencia or at the Canvas on Ninth Avenue. Maybe I'll haunt North Beach and visit the Trieste. Maybe I'll take a stroll and run into some new café, one that only yesterday was a stamp shop or a sushi bar. I wish I had accomplished more; but tomorrow I will accomplish a little. I would make the same attempt in Boise or Budapest, but I'm glad that I find myself, soul in throat, in San Francisco.

30.

TEACHING AT JANE'S

I'VE BEEN TEACHING AT JANE'S for the past three or four years. Some writers teach at great universities or at world-renowned retreat centers. I teach in Jane's quirky Bernal Heights cottage that is guarded by a cat and that features bathroom doors that don't quite lock and a living room decorated with stiletto heels and erotic prints. At which venue would you rather teach? I think it's no contest.

One of the odd results of teaching for Jane is that I see myself everywhere I go. Jane tacks up flyers to announce her classes, and she is relentless in posting them. So when I enter my café, grocery store, or gift shop, there I am, smiling back at me in a fifteen-year-old headshot that I had taken when my first nonfiction book was published. I have seen that face a lot! I know it better than the face I see in the mirror, and as long as I continue using that ancient headshot, I am guaranteed that I will never age. So I tell myself.

Jane's enterprise is called writingsalons.com (with an "s," as she must always remind folks). She offers a wide variety of classes, sponsors student readings in her living room (readings that are suffocating, because hundreds fill a space meant for twenty), and has recently branched out into another country: Berkeley. As a result of this expansion I sometimes teach in my neighborhood, which involves only a stroll, and sometimes I cross the bridge, which nowadays is an eye-popping experience, as a second Bay Bridge (costing billions and billions) is rising up beside the current one.

Jane's cottage has two "classrooms." One is a basement room next to the cramped quarters of a gentleman lodger who emerges from his narrow digs by way of a curtain that opens into the basement kitchen. This ghostly fellow pays part of his rent by helping Jane with classroom tasks, like heating the kettle and turning out the lights, so it is not unusual to trip over him at break or to hear the door lock behind us when we leave. We are used to him and know that he is a friendly ghost.

The second "classroom" is Jane's living room upstairs. I teach from the window seat to students ensconced in love seats and mismatched chairs. It is a charming cottage living room eclectically furnished and lovingly lit. Jane is the ghost on this floor; her curtained bedroom abuts the living room. Usually she is away, but sometimes she is there and will pop out from behind her curtain to peek in and smile. She, too, is a friendly ghost.

The class I've taught most often is called "The Art of the Book Proposal." Folks come to learn what a nonfiction book proposal contains and entails. By the fourth or fifth week, half the students have vanished. They had hoped that the book proposal would demand less of them. The group of thirteen shrinks to a mere six or seven. No matter. The only problem the remaining souls face is how quickly the task of bringing in snacks comes around. The only problem for me is that I grow a little sad, knowing that those who jumped ship have disappointed themselves, no doubt for the umpteenth time.

The first night all is possibility. At the end of the evening, I assign a little homework. The second night two or three people are missing. Possibility has begun its inexorable slide into difficulty. We talk about things like building a platform, preparing a marketing plan, researching the territory that the writer's book will inhabit, articulating the writer's credentials. The next week the class is a little slimmer. A few people are still enthusiastic. For many, resignation has set in.

They are nevertheless happy at break, even the resigned ones. The break is a time for cookies, tea, gossip, and the pleasant ease of Jane's space. The gathered writers enjoy the warmth of the cottage, the artifacts, the conviviality. How humane the break is! But then, like the drill sergeant I once was, I must drag them back to the tasks of the book proposal, to the soliciting of endorsements, to the annotating of the table of contents, to the choosing of a sample chapter to write. The bliss of the break is quickly a distant memory.

Each new class starts on the same high note. But even there, right at the beginning, shadows already intrude: two or three people will come late, one or two will be absent. These early casualties are already wrestling with themselves, doubting themselves, wishing they had signed up for yoga instead. They are already disengaging. Sometimes one will act aghast, as if she had no idea that I might suggest that participants work on their book proposal in a book proposal class. This aghast reaction is invariably a prelude to the demand of a refund. Jane is prepared for this; her refund policy has been hammered on the anvil of a hundred such regrets and denials.

Jane's very San Francisco cottage industry is a blessing. Countless would-be writers have amputated that "would-be" in the cozy confines of her basement or her living room. Short stories, screenplays, and science fiction novels have materialized. Yes, many writers came face-to-face with themselves and fled from the encounter. And indeed, all that fleeing finally wore me out. Though I still teach for Jane, nowadays I only teach one-day workshops. But the balance must tip in favor of calling Jane's enterprise a rousing success. If proof were needed, here it is: every semester a hundred writers risk suffocation to hear one another read.

31

I CAN NO LONGER FIND THE REFERENCE, but I once read somewhere that the imperfections one sees in Victorian windows are known as apple seeds. This being San Francisco, with its period and restored Victorians, many such imperfections are on public view. We are a town of apple seeds.

We are also, because of our Japanese connection, a town quite familiar with the idea of wabi-sabi, the Zen aesthetic that reminds us that nothing lasts, that nothing is finished, and that nothing is perfect. Wry and sorrowful, serene and melancholy, we who honor wabi-sabi work to let go of our longing that life live up to its reputation.

Intellectually, you and I are easy with the wisdom of apple seeds and wabi-sabi. We understand that a novel of ours may appear with three typos, a plot lapse, and a leaden minor character. Intellectually, we accept this, just as we accept that a hundred thousand books appear each year to swallow up our small offering, that the editor who loves us may leave her publishing house and start selling real estate, that the idea that made so much sense in a dream at dawn looks horrid on the page. We know to detach, to forgive the universe, to smile. These things we know.

Viscerally, however, we can hardly tolerate such shortfalls. They make us want to scream. They make us want to tear out our hair. They make us want to murder. They drive us mad. One small example: the early-twentieth-century Lithuanian-born, Paris-based expressionist painter Chaim Soutine. Plagued by the poor quality of his cheap pigments, Soutine would regularly call up a new collector to see if the painting the collector had recently purchased was cracked yet. Often it was. Soutine, intent on repainting it, would demand it back. If the collector refused, suspicious that Soutine had a higher bidder for the painting, Soutine would throw a fit, trembling, turning pale, foaming at the mouth, and suffering a seizure.

Not very Zen. But very human! Our (Western) heart hungers for masterpieces, excellence, immortality, pigments that don't crack, novels that stay in print. We want symphonies made up of four fine movements and dancers who do not fall and break our spell. Our (Western) heart believes in museums, bookstores, CDs, and other valiant efforts at making the ephemeral long lasting. Our (Western) heart, at war with our (Eastern) mind, hates the first dent our new car receives. Our (Eastern) mind knew it was coming but still couldn't adequately prepare us for it.

Maybe that is just as well. Maybe too fine a taste for wabi-sabi and apple seeds is a recipe for despair. Maybe there is actually some grave danger in bowing down before the altars of impermanence and imperfection. Japan has one of the highest suicide rates in the world, and its online suicide groups are exceedingly popular. Does the Japanese citizen, well versed in wabi-sabi, suffering the poignant longing that arises from the knowledge that dust and ashes await, begin to lose his reasons for living? Are the cracks in the vase, the out-of-print books, and the faded tapestries nails in a coffin that begins to look not only inevitable but also attractive? Could be.

Someone said to me the other day, "The illusion of meaning is a prerequisite for choosing to live." That's very likely. I want this book to have meaning for you. I do not want to fall asleep imagining it already gone from the universe and me with it. I would rather picture it in nice piles in mammoth bookstores and in your hands as you visit San Francisco. I would rather picture life, that is, rather than death; the beauty in this book, rather than the flaws; the cookies still to come, rather than the aftermath of crumbs.

Doesn't depression dog the Buddhist, who is just a little too savvy about and sympathetic toward the reality of an eternity without us? Doesn't his warning that we should strive less, desire less, and embrace nothingness create the very pain that he believes is the bedrock of existence? Wouldn't he be better off beginning his next novel, so as to give himself a little pleasure? Certainly a very fine void awaits us; but today we could write up a storm, relish our thousand words, and not worry that seventeen of them could have been more artfully chosen.

Nothing lasts, if eternity is the measure. But what a measure! This book is lasting long enough for you to read it, which is something. We are surrounded, after all, by things that have survived, like mad kings' castles, plays from the 1500s, cave paintings from prehistory, and our photos from childhood. That is not the same as permanence; but, on a human scale, it is a lot to rejoice in. No, eternity mustn't be the measure — eternity is just too severe and absolute a way of measuring.

Maybe nothing is finished, nothing is perfect, and nothing lasts. Or maybe everything is finished, everything is perfect, and everything lasts. More pertinently, maybe neither is the right way to address the universe. Maybe the right way to address the universe is exactly the way you addressed it when you were six and wise, when you sat down and wrote out a story and then illustrated it. You weren't thinking perfect, you weren't thinking imperfect, you were only thinking, "How much fire does a fire-breathing dragon breathe?"

It is good to honor wabi-sabi, insofar as honoring it allows us to accept the cracks in our cherished vase and the typos in our cherished book. But we must not honor it too much, if, by overdoing it, we allow the meaning to leak out of life. It is the road to sadness to see only the warts on the heel and not the curve of the foot, to contemplate a million out-of-print books rather than the book we are breathing into existence. Like wasabi, that fiery Japanese horseradish, a little wabi-sabi goes a long way.

SITE SPECIFIC

THIS IS THE SECOND in what I hope will be a quixotic series of site-specific lessons for writers. (The first was *A Writer's Paris.*) I am taken by the idea that writing, while flowing directly from personality, is also informed in rich ways by the physical locations that get under a writer's skin. Human beings are embodied and encamped: we are flesh-and-blood creatures living in this or that hut or palace. Place matters.

I can tell by the way that Brooklyn and Manhattan still inhabit me that I will have to do *A Writer's New York.* I look forward to taking you from Brooklyn Heights to Coney Island, a nice eleven-mile walk, as we chat about the writing life. I would like to anchor a book in Dublin, another in Budapest, another in Tokyo. The light and shadows of each place, its particular gypsies and outcasts, the Zen and neon of Tokyo, the sour cherries and chess cafés of Budapest, the troubadours and Troubles of Dublin, would ignite different musings and different lessons.

I also have another agenda in writing these books. A key to a long, productive writing life is finding ways to support that life, emotionally and existentially. One such way is to fly off to a stop on the bohemian international highway for a writing sojourn. You honor your writing life by strolling through Barcelona or Prague and stopping every so often to write.

This sort of mindful trip, lasting a week, two weeks, a month, or as long as you can manage, is a tonic that helps you fall back in love with and recommit to your writing. Going to Paris or San Francisco to drink or to shop is not what I have in mind. Going to write is. You go with a light suitcase and a clear intention. You don't even need a guidebook, since you are not a tourist. It won't matter what museums you miss or what restaurants you fail to eat in. Your agenda is blessedly simple: you stroll the streets of a great city and stop every so often to write.

The strolling is important, since city-strolling is the walking meditation of the writer. Get up each day, dress warmly (cities are chilly in the morning), head straight to your first café, have your first cup of coffee and your pumpkin muffin (or *brioche* or *kolache*), and begin writing. Stay put for an hour. Then walk. Something good for your novel, your poem, your screenplay, or your nonfiction book will settle upon you as you stroll. When it settles, hurry onto a bench or into the nearest café. If you have chosen a stop on the bohemian international highway, a café is sure to be nearby.

The scenery doesn't have to be spectacular. Here is the walk I would take from where I live. I'd turn right out my door and walk up and over Bernal Hill, down Folsom Street, and along block after block of Edwardians, Victorians, and Latin life. I'd stroll under freeway overpasses and meander through the outskirts of downtown, where not much is beautiful but everything is interesting.

I'd head all the way to the Embarcadero and the Bay, turn left, and stop at the Ferry Building, a former ferry terminal now revamped and boutiqued. There I'd get coffee and a pastry and take them out to a bench overlooking the Bay; soon I'd be writing. After not too long the morning chill would stop me. I'd pack up and head toward North Beach, a handful of blocks away, and wander the streets around Jackson Square, whose old brick buildings are beautiful but scary — think earthquake. In North Beach I'd choose a café from among the many suitable for writing. Today, let's make it Caffé Trieste, that old standby, for nostalgia's sake.

Having written, I'd head through Chinatown, past the lacquered ducks and the backscratchers, past the spot where Yun Gee and the Chinese Revolutionary Artists' Club hosted a Diego Rivera reception. (The event was rather a cultural catastrophe, since Diego spoke Spanish, French, and Russian but not Chinese, and the tiny square stools, fit for a slim Chinese, did not suit his massive frame, causing one guest to quip that he "overflowed on all sides"). I'd head toward Union Square, stopping, I think, at the mega-Borders, to see which, if any, of my books were currently available.

The café there is a fine spot to write in. Then over the top of Nob Hill, past the Mark Hopkins, to commemorate that long-ago bit of lying, then down the hill past the painted lady of that literary agent couple, to reflect on Christmases past and the horror of fiction proposals. Then on to Mission Street and points south, to the world of winos, leather bars, and modern art, stopping perhaps to get disoriented at the San Francisco Museum of Modern Art.

Then back along Folsom Street or a parallel street, maybe Harrison or Mission, stopping at a Starbuck's or that new café that just opened, to do some last writing. Then straight down Mission and a left on Cortland, all the way home to the Chaise Lounge, to see if it'd opened yet. If it had, one Coppola Merlot, please.

This is a good writing day in San Francisco. If you come, if you fan the flame of your writing desire, and if you hold the intention to write, you can have a good writing day, too. The fog may roll in; the day may prove as chilly as Mark Twain predicted; and you may need a hot drink or two by nightfall. But you will have written. How fine is that?

※

Notes

2. THE BOHEMIAN INTERNATIONAL HIGHWAY

Page 6: *The idea of bohemia caught the imaginations of writers...* Nancy J. Peters, "The Beat Generation and San Francisco's Culture of Dissent," in *Reclaiming San Francisco*, ed. James Brook, Chris Carlsson, and Nancy J. Peters (San Francisco: City Lights Books, 1998), 199.

3. SOUTH OF MARKET

Page 11: *"And there's my room, small, gray..."* Jack Kerouac, "October in the Railroad Earth," in *San Francisco Stories: Great Writers on the City*, ed. John Miller (San Francisco: Chronicle Books, 1990), 143.

8. EARTHQUAKE COUNTRY

Pages 30–31: *"In every direction from the ferry building..."* Jerome B. Clark, quoted in "The San Francisco Earthquake, 1906," EyeWitness to History, http://www.eyewitnesstohistory.com (1997; accessed April 2006).

Pages 31 and 32: *"On Thursday morning,..."* and *"On Mission Street..."* Jack London, "The Fire," in *San Francisco Stories: Great Writers on the City*, ed. John Miller (San Francisco: Chronicle Books, 1990), 245 and 250.

10. CITY LIGHTS

Page 39: *"Ferlinghetti loved the idea of a bookstore..."* Bill Morgan, in *The Beat Generation in San Francisco: A Literary Tour*, ed. Bill Morgan and Lawrence Ferlinghetti (San Francisco: City Lights Books, 2003).

11. AT THE CHAISE LOUNGE

Page 42: *"a chain smoker with a slight mustache, . . . "* Liz Smith, "When Love Was the Adventure," *Time*, June 14, 1999, http://www.time.com/time/time100/heroes/romances/ romances2.html (accessed April 2006).

Page 42: *"Soon after we returned to San Francisco . . ."* Alice B. Toklas, *What Is Remembered* (New York: North Point Press, 1985).

17. THE PERFECT LANDLORD

Page 66: *"At the Handy Colony, . . ."* Andrea Lynn, in a review of George Hendrick and Don Sackrider, *James Jones and the Handy Writers' Colony* (Carbondale, IL: South Illinois University Press, 2001) for the University of Illinois at Urbana Champaign News Bureau, http://www.news.uiuc.edu/gentips/01/05handy.html (accessed April 2006).

Page 68: *"The enchantment of Macondray Lane . . ."* Mick Sinclair, *San Francisco: A Cultural and Literary History* (Northhampton, MA: Interlink Books, 2004), 95.

22. KIPLING AND DESIRE

Pages 85 and 88: *"I am hopelessly in love . . ."* and *"I cannot write connectedly . . ."* Rudyard Kipling, "In San Francisco," in *San Francisco Stories: Great Writers on the City*, ed. John Miller (San Francisco: Chronicle Books, 1990), 138 and 141.

27. A SINGLE KOAN

Page 106: *"What is the true meditation? . . ."* *The Zen Master Hakuin: Selected Writings*, trans. Philip B. Yampolsky (New York: Columbia University Press, 1971; reprint, 1973), 58.

Index of Place-Names

About the Author and Artist

ERIC MAISEL, PHD, is the author of more than thirty works of fiction and nonfiction. His nonfiction titles include *Coaching the Artist Within, Fearless Creating, The Van Gogh Blues, The Creativity Book, Performance Anxiety,* and *A Writer's Paris.* A columnist for *Art Calendar* magazine and a regular contributor to *Artist's Sketchbook* magazine, *Writer's Digest* magazine, and *The Writer* magazine, Maisel is a creativity coach and creativity coach trainer who presents keynote addresses and workshops nationally and internationally.

Maisel holds undergraduate degrees in philosophy and psychology, Master's degrees in counseling and creative writing, and a doctorate in counseling psychology. He is also a California-licensed marriage and family therapist. He lives with his family in San Francisco.

Visit www.ericmaisel.com to learn more about Dr. Maisel, or drop him a line at ericmaisel@hotmail.com.

PAUL MADONNA's strip, *All Over Coffee,* appears weekly in the *San Francisco Chronicle* and on the *Chronicle*'s website, www.SFGate.com. In 2005, he collaborated with the writers' center 826 Valencia to create San Francisco's first Literary Map. His drawings and prints are widely exhibited and can be found in various publications and on his website, www.paulmadonna.com. He lives with his wife in San Francisco.